ISBN 978-1-330-11734-7
PIBN 10029961

This book is a reproduction of an important historical work. Forgotten Books uses
state-of-the-art technology to digitally reconstruct the work, preserving the original format
whilst repairing imperfections present in the aged copy. In rare cases, an imperfection in
the original, such as a blemish or missing page, may be replicated in our edition. We do,
however, repair the vast majority of imperfections successfully; any imperfections that
remain are intentionally left to preserve the state of such historical works.

# 1 MONTH OF
# FREE
# READING

## at
## www.ForgottenBooks.com

By purchasing this book you are eligible for one month membership to ForgottenBooks.com, giving you unlimited access to our entire collection of over 700,000 titles via our web site and mobile apps.

To claim your free month visit: www.forgottenbooks.com/free29961

# Similar Books Are Available from
# www.forgottenbooks.com

THE

# DIFFICULTIES OF THE SOUL;

OR,

# HINDRANCES TO BELIEVING.

BY

W. HAY M. H. AITKEN, M.A.,

Late incumbent of Christ Church, Everton.

Author of "The School of Grace," "What is your Life," etc.

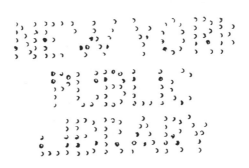

New York:

ANSON D. F. RANDOLPH & COMPANY.

900 Broadway, cor. 20th Street.

# PREFACE.

THE following pages may be said to contain the results of observation and experience in evangelizing work extending over a period of many years. They are offered in the hope that they may to some little extent meet a need which is, I am persuaded, widely felt and often expressed. Many books exist which deal more or less fully with the soul's difficulties; but some of these devote only a slender portion of their contents to this subject, while others employ their whole space with the consideration of only certain parts of the whole subject. The most valuable little book of the kind that I ever remember reading, and one to which I am indebted for the idea of the method which I have adopted in the later chapters of

B

this book, that, namely, of introducing various difficulties in the very words in which they are frequently
stated, has long since, I believe, been out of print;
and I am not able to trust to my recollection either
of its title or the name of its author. Like several
other less methodical books of the same kind, it
was the work of a Nonconformist; and, therefore,
perhaps its excellent and sensible thoughts were
scarcely clothed in a form that would have proved
acceptable to most Church-people, whether lay or
clerical. Other books dealing with this subject,
and amongst them the very useful little work
whose title I inadvertently appropriated when this
treatise first appeared in the pages of the *Clergyman's Magazine,* address themselves mainly, if not
exclusively, to the case of the anxious inquirer, and
do not propose to offer practical suggestions to
him who seeks to give help to such an one. My
object, on the other hand, has been a double one:
I have sought to offer the benefit of any amount
of experience gained by years of evangelizing
work, to my brethren in the ministry, and also

to assist those who are themselves the victims of spiritual perplexity.

With respect to the former of these objects, I have only to say that if to any of my reverend brethren I seem to have taken too much upon me, even in venturing to contemplate it, my apology must be that I am persuaded that experience is the great teacher in work of this order; and he who lays aside, at any rate for a time, the higher and perhaps more skilled labour of the pastor in order to devote himself entirely to the work of an Evangelist, is likely to have more experience of this kind than another whose work is more diversified, though certainly not less exalted. The Evangelist has much to learn from the student and from the pastor; may not student and pastor have something, at any rate, to learn from the Evangelist. I must frankly admit, that in the course of my wanderings hither and thither, I have not unfrequently been much pained by observing the apparent helplessness of some of my brethren in the ministry in dealing with awakened souls; and this I have attributed to the fact, that amidst their many pastoral duties they have to some extent overlooked the most elementary part of their work, and have forgotten St. Paul's advice to Timothy, to "do the work of an Evangelist." If to any such these lessons learnt in the school of experience should prove of service, I shall feel that my time and labour will not have been misspent.

With respect to the other object, I can only say that I have written with the deepest feeling of sympathy for those whose case I contemplate. Yet, with a strong and sorrowful conviction of the reality of many of the difficulties to which I refer, I have also an inward persuasion, that however grave these may seem, none of them are insurmountable; but that, like the clouds which seem to line the horizon with vast mountain barriers, they only need to be resolutely approached in order to be dispersed into empty nothingness.

Very conscious of the many imperfections of my treatment of a subject as full of deep interest as it is important, I none the less commit this little effort to help those who most of all need help into the gracious hands of the great Lord of the harvest, beseeching Him, if it be His will, to use it for His glory and for the benefit of those whose case it is designed to reach.

*Holmeside, Hazelwood, Derby.*

# CONTENTS.

## CHAPTER VI.

## CHAPTER VII.

## CHAPTER VIII.

## CHAPTER IX.

## CHAPTER X.

## CHAPTER XI.

## CHAPTER XII.

# CHAPTER I.

IT is a notable feature in the moral economy
of the world, that God has ordained that for
the most part man shall be the means of conveying
spiritual blessing from God to his fellow-man. The
object of this Divine ordinance it is not difficult to
discover. It is the will of God that His Church
should be what the human family might have been
had man never fallen,—not a mere aggregation of
individuals, but an organic whole, compacted
together by the mutual relations of its parts, and
pervaded throughout by a lively sympathetic sensibility. The mere fact that in the reception of
our first spiritual impressions we are for the most
part indebted to our fellow-men, contributes to this
end. We "love the brethren" because in the first
instance we owe so much to their brotherly care.

But more than this, it is the will of God that the Church of Christ should be the reflex of His own moral image, and especially that she should resemble Him in the exercise of the highest and most unselfish benevolence. But the fact that we are ourselves so much indebted to others tends to induce on our part a disposition to love and benefit our kind; whereas, did we all receive our spiritual blessings direct from the hand of God, we might naturally be disposed to conclude that others would be certain to receive them after a similar fashion, and thus the first motive of a life of Christian benevolence would be withdrawn, and, we may add, one great benefit of social existence would be forfeited.

This thought of our interdependence on one another has a most solemn side. How much it adds to the gravity of life's responsibilities! Looking at these things from man's point of view, the happiness and well-being of our fellow-creatures, the extension of light and knowledge to hearts darkened by unbelief and blighted by sin, rests with us; so that when we are living lives of indolent carelessness, we are actually, so far as in us lies, shutting the door of mercy in the face of mankind, and exposing ourselves to a terrible accusation, when the voice of our brother's blood shall rise up against us into the ears of God. On the other hand, there are few thoughts that tend so much as this to bring forcibly before our minds the dignity of our nature, and the wonderful privileges which belong to our present position in God's universe. God will not as a rule work without us ; but He is willing to work with us in such wise that the results shall tell for all eternity. Surely the unfallen intelligences of glory might almost envy us (were envy possible amongst angels) the privilege which we enjoy of entering into direct communication with and exercising a personal influence upon those who are far from God, while we endeavour as with a brother's hand to lead them back into the paths of peace.

Of course this thought of our dependence on each other has to be duly balanced by the consideration of God's sovereign power, and of His ability to act in the moral universe as He pleases. There are doubtless instances in which the action of God upon the human heart is perfectly direct and immediate, and without the intervention of any human agents. Such cases are no doubt per mitted to guard us against peril of superstition and prevent us from attributing to man that which belongs to God alone. They also supply us with an answer to those who (as specially in our day) would be only too ready to attribute the moral phenomena of spiritual influence to some such physical force as we indicate by the term "animal magnetism."

Even in such exceptional cases, however, we have to bear in mind how much of preparatory work has been wrought through man before the voice of God sounds directly in the human heart; and it must be admitted that such cases are rare.

As a rule, it is through man that man is blessed. It was so in primitive times; it is so still. The Ethiopian eunuch may be interested in the writings of the prophet Isaiah, and ponder with inquiring mind upon the mysteries which that wondrous roll contains; but the prophecy of the ancient seer needs to be supplemented by the living voice of a Philip before light dawns on the inquirer's mind. The earnest and gifted Apollos, already partially acquainted with Christian truth, requires to be more fully instructed by personal communication with Aquila and Priscilla. The brethren found by St. Paul at Ephesus, who are already in a certain sense believers, have to thank the straightforward and searching inquiry of the great Apostle for the reception of a fuller and deeper spiritual blessing, and apparently for the commencement of a new life in their hearts. Perhaps the most striking illustration of this rule, of all that the New Testament contains, is the case of Cornelius. Here we observe two distinct miraculous manifestations are permitted, not in order to bring the truth of God directly home to the Roman centurion's heart, but in order to bring a human agent into the presence of the man to whom he was to be a messenger of life. Cornelius knew much of the power of prayer, yet the revelation of Gospel truth was not given to him directly by the Holy Spirit of God in answer to his prayer. A wonderful vision of an angel was granted to him, but the lips of the angel were sealed to the message which might in one moment have conveyed life and peace to the centurion's heart. Simon Peter would have been so reluctant to undertake this particular service, that another miracle had to be performed in order to dispose him to accept the invitation from the Gentile soldier. All this, just to bring an anxious inquirer within reach of human help!

If such is the importance which God seems to attach to this law of His moral economy in this world, we shall not be wrong in entertaining a correspondingly strong opinion of its wisdom and necessity.

The *"Mission"* movement in the Church of England has prominently drawn attention to one particular point which comes under the great truth of the interdependence of man on man. It has been proved over and over again in missions, that whereas the public preaching of the Word from the pulpit to the multitude is the means which God most frequently employs to awaken the careless and indifferent to a sense of their true position, and to dispose them to seek after salvation; on the other hand, and no less obviously, it is for the most part personal conference with the individual which is the means that God honours to lead the awakened soul into the enjoyment of peace and the consciousness of pardon. To this circumstance is to be attributed the great stress which all really successful mission preachers lay upon the *"After-meeting,"* and the point that they make of so arranging that meeting as to give some opportunity for personal conference with those who are anxiously seeking after God.

The extent to which this is the case continues to be a matter of surprise even to those who have had much experience **in** mission work. Again and again they have occasion to notice that where the clearest and most powerful statements from the pulpit fail to reach the case of particular souls, a few plain words uttered in conversation will remove the difficulties that have been encumbering the way to the cross, and lead to the immediate acceptance of God's gift of peace and pardon. Nay, more than this, they often have to observe that the very errors and sins which they have been zealously denouncing and exposing from the pulpit will be illustrated by the experiences of the after-meeting. The preacher has perhaps been inveighing against some common forms of self-righteousness, behind which so many conceal themselves, and exposing the error of the man who flatters himself that all is well because "he has never done any particular harm to anybody;" he comes down from the pulpit, and perhaps the first person that he accosts in the after-meeting will make use of this very expression. Or he has been pointing out the necessity of looking to Christ as the only basis of our confidence, and the danger of attempting to rest upon our own frames and feelings; probably he will not have been working long in the after-meeting before he meets with some one who introduces the word *feel* into every second sentence that he utters. That this is actually the case, and that I am not drawing an exaggerated picture, every experienced mission preacher will allow.

If asked for the reason ot this, we may reply that in the first place people do not, as a rule, when hearing a sermon, begin by listening for themselves; rather they begin by listening to a preacher as they would to a political orator. It does not occur to them at first that it is their own case that is being described, their sins or errors that are being exposed to view. Nor is this all, there is a certain apparently natural perversity which belongs to man, which I always think is in itself one of the strongest and most startling proofs of the reality of the operations of the spirit of darkness. The result of his influence upon the human heart is that we are for the most part least ready to accept that particular truth which is most specially adapted to and required by our own case. How often do we find that a totally unawakened man will listen with apparent readiness to statements respecting the love and goodness of God, but practically close his ears when the preacher endeavours to probe his own conscience and con vict him of sin. How many awakened souls listen with equal avidity to the thunders of the law, when what they need is to accept the comforts of the Gospel, till they find themselves sinking deeper and deeper into despondency, or approaching despair,_as the words of terror sink into their ears and overwhelm their hearts; while they seem to shut their ears when the message of God's love in Christ—the very thing that they need to listen to —is pressed upon them. Thus it often happens that people go away with a lively impression upon their minds of just those particular parts of the discourse which were least suited to their case. All this is changed when you come to deal with the individual; you can then select the line of conversation which you consider to be most appropriate to the particular case, nay, you can exclude all others from immediate consideration.

There is this further to be said, that in direct conversation with an awakened soul you are able not merely to explain the truth and clear away difficulties in a manner that is impossible from the pulpit, but you can also use a certain gentle personal pressure to induce an immediate surrender of the heart to Christ, and acceptance of the blessings which He offers. In the case of Philip and the eunuch the proposal of immediate action came from the inquirer, and sometimes it does so still, but more frequently experience teaches that this suggestion has to be made by the Christian helper, and that in the case of true and earnest inquirers after Christ, it is in a large number of instances responded to with alacrity.    But the proposal has to be made.    "And now why tarriest thou?" exclaimed the messenger Ananias to the stricken Saul of Tarsus, in that memorable *after-meeting* in the little room in the street called Strait.    The sermon which produced conviction of sin had been preached on the road, when the flash of glory burst upon the man's astonished gaze, and the voice of the risen Christ sounded through his trembling heart.    But even in this case it was as in so many others, the Saviour Himself would not take the work of carrying the glad tidings of great joy to that stricken one out of the hands of His faithful servants.    So Ananias has to enter into personal conversation with Saul, to remove his difficulties, to assure him of God's willingness to pardon the past and to blot out even such a stain as the blood of Stephen had left on the persecutor's hands, and the messenger, like a true helper, is careful to bring things to a point, and to press the message home with the question, "Why tarriest thou?"

Even so it is still; when doubts have been resolved, and misapprehensions cleared away, it becomes possible for us to suggest to the inquiring soul the expediency of immediate action, and there and then in a large number of cases the decision is actually made, and the first step in the spiritual life is taken.

But " who is sufficient for these things ? " how much of wisdom, of delicacy on the one hand, and strength on the other, of incisive faithfulness or tender sympathy, is needed by the man who would be a real help, and in no respects a hindrance to his fellow-sinner when approaching the cross of Christ! Unquestionably it is only the direct assistance of the Holy Spirit of God that can make us truly efficient in work of this kind; at the same time we must remember that it is His wont to work through human agencies in this as in other respects, and we may be taught by Him through the experience of others. Some of us, from the nature of our work, are likely to be more familiar than others with the difficulties of the awakened soul, and should therefore be the better skilled in dealing with them. From such, other less ex-perienced workers may learn much that may be of service to them in their attempts to be useful to

others, and it is with this thought on my mind that
I offer the following pages on the subject of the
difficulties and perplexities which beset the soul
in its approach to the cross of Christ.   In these I
shall endeavour to deal in detail with the various
phases of spiritual experience through which we
find that men pass ere they enter upon the full
enjoyment of that happy life of settled peace and
calm repose in God, which it is the birthright of
every true Christian to enjoy.   My hope in writing
on this important subject is twofold—first, that
this volume may be of some little service to
those who are themselves engaged in the delicate
and difficult task of leading souls to Christ; and
secondly, that if it should fall into the hands of
any who are themselves depressed by the difficulties to which I shall refer, God may be pleased
to use my words to their spiritual comfort and
deliverance.

# CHAPTER II.

OUR subject introduces us to the human soul at that point in its experience at which the man passes from a state of apathetic unconcern to a state of honest inquiry and earnest desire. Before this point is reached, the soul knows nothing of *difficulties* from personal experience, and therefore can make no effort to grapple with them. The unawakened soul may either form an exaggerated estimate of the difficulties which bar the way of access to the great Father of spirits, or he may be persuaded that none of any kind exist, but in either case his conduct will be the same. If he believes the difficulties to be insurmountable, it is not because he has made an honest attempt to surmount them, but because he wishes to be saved the trouble of such an effort; "the sluggard saith there is a lion in the way." If he believes that the way of salvation is easy and devoid of hindrances, he finds in this a reason why he should put off all consideration of such matters till a more convenient season, possibly to a dying hour. But when a man is really in earnest, he can no longer rest satisfied, either with a vague apprehension that the difficulties are manifold, or with a superficial assurance that none at all exist. He is bent upon the acquisition of some real and actual benefit, and will neither be defeated by trifling obstacles, nor put off with conventional counterfeits, and then it is that he finds to his cost that the soul has its difficulties.

It is this feature of our subject which invests it with such a special and we may say such a sorrowful interest. It seems at first a sad and inexplicable fact, that the soul should not only have its infirmities, its sorrows, and its sins; but that even when it seeks to turn from these it should be faced by difficulties—real, grave, discouraging difficulties—and should have to fight its way through these into the enjoyment of God's peace. In our subsequent experience the explanation comes, and we learn to thank God for early trials from which we have gained so much. The seed once sown in tears brings forth its fruit, and we reap our harvest perhaps in a more reasonable and intelligent faith ; perhaps in a habit of calm moral confidence in God, independent of emotional fluctuations; perhaps in a peculiar delicacy of sympathy for others who pass through similar trials ; perhaps in an increased value for, and in a disposition the more jealously to guard, that which we obtained at the cost of so much suffering ; or if not thus, yet in some other way, God's dealings with the seeking soul will. be in measure justified now, and more fully vindicated hereafter.

But here a question presents itself as to what is the true view of these difficulties. Are we to regard them as directly ordained by God, and as an integral part of the economy of grace, a necessary element in the discipline of love, whereby the wandering soul is to be led into the way of peace? or are we to regard them as the product of the machinations of the malignant spirits of darkness, and the proof of their baneful influence over the heart of man? or are we to regard them as self-caused, the fruit of ignorance or perversity on the part of those who are themselves the victims of their own folly?

It may be observed that these explanations of

the phenomena of spiritual difficulty are not **neces-sarily** exclusive of each other. It is conceivable that the perplexities of the soul are to be attributed in a greater or less degree to all these causes com-bined, or that the true explanation may vary in different cases. But as a right understanding of the possible and probable causes of such difficulties is the first step towards their removal, we shall not err in spending a little time on the consideration of each of these positions, endeavouring to ascer-tain in what manner the awakened soul is affected by the attitude which God maintains towards him, by the malevolent influence of the tempter, or by the frailty and blindness of human nature.

The first of these explanations is that which the *heart* of man is generally most ready to adopt, even though the mind may find some difficulty in admitting it. Hence while it is only rarely that we hear people attribute their spiritual embarrassment in definite terms to the inexplicable caprice of an unsympathising God, we are painfully familiar with language which implies as much as this, though it does not explicitly state it. Such assertions, when they are made, are usually the expressions of a certain irreverent petulance—the peevishness of a spoilt child—rather than the grave utterance of a moral conviction. But far more subtle, and therefore more dangerous than any such overt impeachment of Divine wisdom and love, is the lurking thought that, inasmuch as we have, according to our own ideas, done all that we could to obtain the blessing we seek, and yet it seems as far from us as ever, it cannot really be God's will that we should obtain it at all. We do not detect where our own fault lies, and so we practically assume that it does not lie with us at all, and thus imply, though we do not assert, that it lies with God.

Nor are there wanting such elements of truth in this view of the case as may afford a plausible basis for the error. It is a personal favour—a spiritual boon which is dependent upon God's attitude towards us—that we are seeking, and if we find it not, it must be because He does not bestow it upon us. From this obvious truth it is easy to pass to the conclusion that He does not bestow it because in His sovereign pleasure He elects not to bestow it, and therefore the soul subsides into a sort of spiritual fatalism, with the feeling that until He chooses to change His mind the benefit must remain unbestowed.

Here again the strength of the error lies in the elements of truth which it at once contains and distorts. It is true that God is a Sovereign, and acts according to His own good pleasure ; but it is also as true that He acts in accordance with *laws,* fixed and unchanging, because they cannot be improved, as that He is totally free from all that we understand by the term arbitrary, and wholly incapable of yielding to blind impulse or caprice. The fact is, that the view that such a soul takes of God is not only untrue, but the exact opposite of the truth. It is not because God acts by caprice, but precisely because He will never do so, that the desired blessing is not obtained. God has offered salvation to all upon certain definite terms, the best and wisest that His infinite love and wisdom could devise : were He to change these terms to suit the caprice of each particular soul, that from one cause or other finds it difficult to accept them, He would Himself be displaying an amount of caprice which must shake the faith in His wisdom and constancy of all intelligent beings. If, on the other hand, He adheres to them, the soul that for one reason or other fails to comply with them must also fail to obtain the blessing it desires until it humbles itself and submits. Hence it is actually true in such cases that God Himself and His wise and just laws are the immediate cause of the difficulty which the soul has to contend with. But the further question has to be answered, What is the reason of this cause? what is it that makes a God whose nature is love, and His laws which must therefore be the expression of love, the immediate cause of difficulty and embarrassment to a seeking soul?

This inquiry leads us to refer to the other two explanations of the phenomena of spiritual difficulty suggested above; and first to consider whether they are attributable to the malignant influence of the evil one, and if so, to examine the grounds for such a conclusion.

Whatever amount of scepticism may exist in our age as to the existence and operations of a mysterious intelligence of evil, it is quite evident to the reader of the New Testament that both our Lord and His disciples were firmly persuaded of both. He only who can find in his own experience no corroborative testimony is free to indulge an honest doubt on this subject, and surely the number of these much-to-be-envied sceptics must needs be small. But taking it for granted that the testimony of the New Testament is trustworthy, it seems very reasonable to conclude, on all grounds, that as it is the first great aim of the Holy Spirit to draw us to Christ, so it will be the first great aim of the spirit of evil to keep us from Him. Our conclusions on this subject are mainly inferential, but they need not on that account be rejected. But little is told us to gratify our curiosity with respect to this great mystery, yet that little suggests much. We read of a spirit that " worketh in the children of disobedience," a word which in several other passages is rendered " unbelief" by our translators, and which stands opposed to and contrasted with " the obedience of faith." This emphatic mention of the prominent moral characteristic of those in whom the spirit of evil works suggests that it is the special workmanship of him who works within them.

Once again, we read that " If our gospel be hid, it is hid to them that are lost : in whom the god of this world hath blinded the minds of them which believe not, lest the light of the glorious gospel of Christ, who is the image of God, should shine unto them." In this remarkable passage it is observed that the great object of the enemy of souls is to prevent the light of the Gospel from shining into the hearts of men. It is further implied that he effects this by rendering men indisposed to faith. It is also worthy of notice that, in speaking of

Christ, the Apostle introduces the words, as of set purpose, " who is the image of God," implying that man is shut off from the knowledge of God when he is blinded to the revelation of Christ, His image. It may be collected, then, from the passage, by its general tone and substance, if not by strict logical inference, first, that Satan seeks to keep souls, above all things, from the Gospel ; secondly, that he does this by suggesting and prompting unbelief ; and thirdly, that he fosters unbelief by presenting false and distorted views of God to the human soul, and using all his influence to divert its vision from Christ, the Interpreter of the Father's heart to His alienated children.

But it is not merely from one or two passages which seem to imply it that we gather the conclusion that much of the difficulty experienced by the awakened soul is the direct result of the baneful influence of the father of lies, exerted with special force at this particular period in human experience. It would seem, indeed, that in the very nature of the case there are the strongest grounds of probability to warrant us in believing that this conclusion corresponds with fact. It is only to be expected that he will employ to the utmost all the malevolent ingenuity that he may be possessed of, in order to keep back the soul from the acceptance of salvation on God's own terms.   He must be aware that his tyrant power over the human heart ends the moment that we approach the cross; and hence, to prevent this, his most sedulous efforts will be directed.   The task of keeping an awakened soul away from Christ would seem to be a task most thoroughly congenial to his malignant character.   It is a work in which all those qualities which we have learnt from Scripture to attribute to Satan are eminently called into play.   The ruthless cruelty of the roaring lion, the subtlety of the old serpent, and, above all, the libellous blasphemies against the character of God in which the father of lies delights; all these, and many similar attributes of the great foe of God and man, are amply illustrated in his dealings with the human heart at such a time.

We remember how, in the days of our Lord's earthly ministry, the evil spirits, on more than one occasion, exhibited a marked reluctance to leave the bodies of their miserable victims; and how, in some cases, they gave special proofs of their fell power just before yielding to the imperious command of One whose superior authority they could not resist.   How often have we beheld such scenes reproduced in the inner experiences of those who are escaping from his yoke, and how grievously lacerated and cruelly ill-used does the soul often appear to be, ere the strong man armed is ejected and the stronger than he divides the spoil.

It seems to me a matter of no small importance that the awakened soul should clearly understand that he is likely to be in a special degree assailed by the spiritual foe the moment that he begins to "turn and seek after God." Half the battle, we may almost say, would be gained if such an one could but truthfully say, "We are not ignorant of his devices;" but the real truth is, that the opposite is usually the case. The transformation of Satan into an angel of light, which so often happens at such times, takes the soul completely by surprise, and leads him in his helpless bewilderment to confuse between the humbling impressions made by the Holy Ghost and the disheartening depressions caused by "the accuser of the brethren." Thus Satan contrives to construct a labyrinth around the Cross, a perfect network of misleading paths ; and as the soul attempts to draw near, the whispered suggestion turns him off now to the right hand and now to the left, and so in very weariness he wanders round and round, ever seeming on the point of reaching the goal, and yet never getting really nearer, until at length, it may be insensibly, he begins to lose ground, and by-and-by the earnest desire is chilled by despair.  The prisoner of hope, the victim of fruitless delays, becomes paralyzed with despondency, and is fain to abandon the search as useless.  It is with him as with Sir Percivale in quest of the Holy Grale :—

> "Then every evil word I had spoken once,
>   And every evil thought I had thought of old,
>   And every evil deed I ever did,
>   Awoke and cried, ' This quest is not for thee !'
>   And lifting up my eyes, I found myself
>   Alone, and in a land of sand and thorns,
>   And I was thirsty even unto death,
>   And I too cried, ' *This quest is not for thee.*' "

# CHAPTER III.

HE who endeavours to help the seeking soul will constantly have to notice how skilfully and with what wondrous versatility of subtle malice the great enemy of souls adapts the form of his attack to the case of those with whom he has to deal; how he turns even some of the most commendable elements of human character to his own account, and makes capital out of our infirmities. All natures, however, are not equally liable to his attacks *at this point* in their spiritual experience. Indeed, the difference between man and man in this respect is truly surprising. Some men seem scarcely conscious of an effort or a struggle in coming to Christ. They receive the truth with the simple confiding faith of little children, the moment that it is clearly set forth before their awakened hearts; and such persons frequently give proof, by their immediate joy and their subsequent constancy, that the change has been a genuine one.

It is a mistake, then, to suppose that long dark hours of spiritual conflict and agony must invariably precede a true conversion. They sometimes do, but they often do not, and this is not because of any friendly disposition on the part of the tempter, but because his knowledge of the human heart leads him to forbear his assaults in cases where they are unlikely to be successful, and to reserve himself for a more favourable opportunity. It is even possible that he has skill enough to discern that the very form of attack which acts so disastrously on one, might be indirectly productive of beneficial effects on another. For, in the case of those who receive the Gospel with little or no difficulty, the chief and most common danger is that the work may be superficial, that the fallow ground of the heart may never be broken up deeply enough to ensure a satisfactory harvest in the future; and in such cases doubts and misgivings, which may lead to introspection, may in the end produce a fuller and truer knowledge of self and sin, and thus may be turned to good account. Those unquestionably escape a good deal of sorrowful and trying experience " who receive the word " at once " with joy "; and it would be well that all should do so; but we should err in supposing that such always make the best Christians, or that they are not exposed to special trials of their own. from which their more timorous brethren, to great extent, escape. Here, indeed, we find ourselves brought face to face with the great law of moral compensation, of which the student of human nature is continually finding illustrations in his observations of the characteristics of individuals, and which we shall probably see at the last great revelation has obtained to a far larger extent than perhaps any of us now dream.

These remarks have prepared the way for the consideration of that third cause of spiritual difficulty, to which we have already referred. It cannot be denied that the character and temperament of the seeking soul, and his inclination to yield to his natural disposition instead of rising above it, are not unfrequently the chief causes of the distress from which he suffers, and of the difficulty which he experiences in obtaining what he seeks. It is indeed impossible to distinguish in all cases between the malignant influence exercised by

Satan and the workings of our natural infirmity or perversity; but it is these natural characteristics that offer a basis of operations to the enemy which he is only too ready to seize and employ for his own ruthless purposes.

It will be found then, as a general rule, that they who suffer most from the attacks of Satan at this particular point in their spiritual experience, are persons of a nervous and somewhat melancholic temperament. Many of the victims of these trying experiences will be scrupulous even to a fault; exceedingly cautious of committing themselves to any statement about themselves that their own feelings do not abundantly justify; laudably jealous of unreality, and yet prone to induce it by the very habit of mind, which leads them to be continually suspecting themselves of it. Almost all who suffer in this way will be intensely subjective, and much given to morbid introspection; in many cases, indeed, this process is carried to such length that the imagination acquires an abnormal activity in the creation of mental illusions, moral spectres, and we may even say horrors, which the perplexed and excited understanding, unduly strained in one particular direction, fails to discriminate from less visionary forms of evil that lurk within. It is easy to see how narrow is the line that divides extreme cases of this class from certain forms of religious insanity; and, indeed, it is not an uncommon thing for a mind otherwise sound, and even robust, to become so warped and unstrung upon this point, as to be almost beyond the reach of reasonable counsel.

There is, perhaps, nothing that illustrates more forcibly the pitiless cruelty of our spiritual foe than the advantage he takes of these natural peculiarities of temperament in order to torment this class of victims. The infirmities that appeal to our sympathy only serve to rouse his malice, and the more ready such persons are to torture themselves, the more triumphantly does he trample them in the dust. Yet we have often had occasion to notice that in many cases he defeats himself, and that those whom he has passed through the hottest fires, make in the end the brightest Christians. The lesson of simple confidence which they were so slow to learn is at last as it were branded on their hearts by the things that they have suffered, and like Thomas of old, they who began by doubting end by rising to higher reaches of faith than are attained by others who have not passed through

an equally severe discipline of conflict and of
sorrow.

There are a few other thoughts which suggest
themselves to our minds before we pass on from
this part of our subject.  In considering the causes
of the difficulties encountered by the awakened
soul, we must take into consideration peculiarities
of education, of religious training, and of outward
circumstances.  Those whose minds have been
from their earliest years familiar with a truth
which their hearts have not accepted, find a special
difficulty in so grasping the message of salvation
as that it shall produce any sensibly real effect
upon their inward experience.  On the other hand,
those who have been wholly devoid of religious
training, and even of serious thought, are so shut
in by the barriers of ignorance, that even when
an interest is excited, much patience is often
needed before they can be brought to discover
the relation of the Gospel message to their own
case.  Hence the great difficulty of dealing effec-
tively with members of the lowest stratum of
society in a brief *mission* extending only over a
few days; or indeed with any, to whatever social
class they may belong, who merit the name of
*outsiders*, people, we mean, who have been leading

an utterly godless and irreligious life. Such persons do not even understand the terms you employ. You speak to them about sin, and repentance, and salvation; but at first you might almost as well address them in another language, so little capable do they seem of grasping the ideas which the words are intended to convey. We are persuaded that this is a much more frequent cause of difficulty to the awakened soul than one might at first be disposed to think, and we would strongly urge those who seek to assist the inquirer, not to take it for granted that such hearers possess an intellectual knowledge of even the most elementary theological truths.

Once again, religious training is often at the root of much spiritual perplexity. We have again and again had occasion to notice the effect of Wesleyan teaching, and above all of Wesleyan practice, on anxious souls who have been brought up under that system. The Church of Christ at large owes an unmeasurable debt of gratitude to that Society, which was the means, we may say, of reviving Evangelical truth throughout our land in a very dark day, and whose members are still amongst the foremost in doing evangelizing work. Yet we are free to say that in many parts of the country, at any rate, so much stress is laid in their teaching upon the importance of the emotional element in religious experience, that many who really desire to be Christians indeed are kept back by their inability to make themselves feel what they hear so much about. It is generally easy to detect those who have been trained in this school by the presence of this characteristic, but it is much harder to disabuse their mind of the idea that some such indescribable emotions are necessary before the soul can trust itself uure-servedly to Christ, or to prevent them from making all sorts of futile efforts to awaken feelings and induce sensations which, if they succeed, will probably be attributable rather to hysterical ex-citement than to real spiritual influences of the Holy Ghost, upon the human heart.

Or to give an illustration from an opposite quarter: The difficulties of the soul are frequently attributable, to a very great extent, to the influence of strong Calvinistic teaching, and that even in cases where Calvinistic doctrines are not pleaded definitely, as they frequently are, (of such cases we shall have to take notice when we come to treat of intellectual difficulties,) as reasons why the soul cannot trust itself to Christ. Men's

minds become insensibly imbued with a conviction
not only of their spiritual helplessness apart from
God, which is a fact, but of their moral incapacity
to respond to the Divine influences and to obey
the Divine call, which is not a fact: and hence,
as our Article well puts it, the devil succeeds in
"thrusting them into desperation." Having heard
so much of God's part in the matter of man's
salvation—how He convicts, gives repentance,
enlightens, enables to believe, fills with joy and
peace, comforts with a conscious assurance of acceptance, preserves from apostacy, and so forth,—
the soul fails to perceive that it too has an important part to perform, and assumes an attitude of
passive waiting, where God calls upon it to exert
all its faculties in repenting and turning to Him.

We may also notice that these difficulties are
in many cases due to special circumstances.
Perhaps the awakened soul has been brought to
think seriously about spiritual things by the sudden
change which he has seen in some acquaintance.
It has not as yet occurred to him that God has
different ways of dealing with different people,
and that because his neighbour happens to have
had experiences of a particular kind he is not
justified in concluding that he must necessarily

3

pass through exactly the same. He has heard one affirm that he felt just as if a light had suddenly shone into his heart; and so he makes up his mind that until he too perceives such a golden illumination he cannot be right with God. Hence he remains waiting, hoping for the light to shine; and not getting what he wants, will not hear of simply trusting to the character and work of Christ.

May it not be that the habit which largely prevails amongst evangelists of describing remarkable cases of conversion, enhances this difficulty? It is natural that we should select the most remarkable cases in order to add interest to our illustrations, but surely we need to beware lest our descriptions should prevent our hearers from receiving the benefit we desire to convey, instead of making plain how they may receive them. During the time of the Irish revival, when so many extraordinary psychical phenomena were arresting the attention of all observers, a very wide-spread feeling began to prevail amongst the country people that a conversion could hardly be genuine unless accompanied by physical prostration and the other unusual features then so prevalent; and we can easily understand how grave an obstacle may thus in many cases have intervened between those who were incapable of being thus affected and the object of their sincere desire.

The remarks which we have here made with respect to these causes of spiritual difficulty which are attributable to the influence of our fellow-men, suggest a suitable answer to those who deprecate all personal interference with the seeking soul, and illustrate in a very practical way our opening observation; for if so much harm may be done by human influence, it surely is only reasonable that man should also be permitted to help. Whilst some, at any rate, are either consciously or unconsciously workers together with Satan in increasing the perplexity of the anxious soul, surely others may be workers together with God's Holy Spirit in endeavouring to relieve it.

In order that we may be the better able to do so, we have dwelt at some length upon the causes of these distressing experiences; for unless we discern whence they proceed we are scarcely likely to be skilful in our treatment of them.

Possibly, too, these pages may meet the eyes of some who are themselves the victims of spiritual perplexities such as we have referred to. To such it will be no small gain if the perusal of what has been said on this subject should lead them to detect the secret source of their misery, either in their reluctance to yield to God's terms of salvation, or in the ruthless assaults of the enemy, or in their disposition to humour their own infirmities and to yield to the depressing influences of a melancholic temperament. For to understand the cause of a disease is the first step towards obtaining a cure; and in spiritual diseases of this class, the detection of the cause is often equivalent to the discovery of the remedy.

Having now endeavoured to throw what light we can upon this part of our subject, it remains that we should consider in detail some of the various forms that the difficulties of the soul may assume, and show how they may best be dealt with, and to this work we shall address ourselves in our subsequent papers.

# CHAPTER IV.

## INTELLECTUAL DIFFICULTIES. DOUBTS AS TO THE TRUTH OF REVELATION.

IN proceeding to consider in detail some of the various forms and phases of religious difficulty with which the inquiring soul may have to contend, we must call attention first of all to a primary and fundamental difference which distinguishes one class of doubters or of seekers, as the case may be, from another. The difficulties of the soul may be either *objective* or *subjective;* they may take the form of tormenting doubts as to the truth of Revelation, or they may take the form of doubts as to whether the Christian Revelation, though assuredly true, is really applicable to the case of the doubter. In referring to the objective perplexities of the soul, we find ourselves in this difficulty; on the one hand we are so painfully conscious that these are a very real hindrance to many, that we feel our treatment of the subject before us would be most incomplete, were we to

make no reference whatever to them; while on the
other hand, to allow ourselves to be drawn aside
into a digression on the Christian evidences would
be to lose sight of the prime object of these pages,
and to waste time and space in a superficial glance
at topics which, if touched upon at all, require to
be fully and methodically treated.

On the whole, it will perhaps be our wisest course
to hazard a few remarks upon this subject; for
who can refuse the deepest and tenderest sympathy
to those who are battling against these adverse
winds, and yet, it may be, from time to time find
themselves cruelly overborne in their struggle with
"the spectres of the mind," and chilled to the
very heart's core by the blight of intellectual unbelief? I do not speak of the willing sceptic who
adopts an infidel profession in order to escape the
reproaches of his conscience or the good counsel
of Christian friends, who rejoices in the thought of
being able to sin with impunity, or who arrogates
to himself an air of superior wisdom highly flattering to his own conceits. Such a man, whatever
his sincerity or insincerity, cannot be described as
an honest and earnest seeker after truth, still less
as an awakened man alive to the seriousness of
the issues at stake. But there are some to whom
doubt is torment, and yet they seem unable to

shake it off; who would give their right hand to know that Christianity is all that it professes to be, and who yet, for some reason or other, cannot satisfy themselves that it is. Yes, there are honest, earnest, gentle-hearted, and sorrowful doubters— only too many—who seem to need our help so sorely, and yet whom, in so many instances, we feel as little able to help as the whole college of Apostles could help one doubting Thomas, until the Lord revealed Himself to him.

It often falls to the lot of the mission-preacher to be approached by such as these, who seem quite as much in earnest as any other inquirers, and yet who seem to have absolutely no point of belief in common with him,—men who feel it highly improbable that there is **a** God, or that they themselves have a soul. The difficulty of dealing with such cases is enhanced by the fact that even in morality we can find no common footing to seize as the base of our operations. The modern materialist is consistent throughout ; he knows no moral code save utilitarianism, and he only judges of sin as the unprofitable or injurious. To what then can we make our appeal ? on what fulcrum can we rest our lever of Gospel truth in order to shake this citadel of unbelief?

In attempting to answer this most difficult question, I am reminded of our blessed Lord's words to His disciples when they asked Him, astonished at their failure, "Lord, why could not we cast him out?" The answer which He gave ("This kind goeth not forth but by prayer and fasting") seems to imply that there are certain forms of spiritual evil which can only be overcome by the presence of extraordinary spiritual power in the hearts of those who meet them. It is very striking how men of much simplicity and little reasoning power are frequently used of God to give the answer in demonstration of the spirit and power, where wisdom of words may often fail. An interesting illustration of this is given in the biography of the Rev. W. Pennefather, recently published. An anonymous correspondent states that, when first he was quite casually brought under Mr. Pennefather's ministry, he became conscious of a power which seemed to sway his whole soul in spite of terrible doubts as to the truth of God's Word, and even as to the existence of God Himself. "That power," continues the writer, "was *the intense reality* of the man who spoke, and the intense reality of the man who *lived* so mightily the truth he proclaimed. Often have I gone into that church with some (as I thought) unanswerable difficulty, and as often have I come away marvelling at the power of God's truth set forth with extreme simplicity, but with a force and unction which carried conviction to my heart." They whose lives are standing testimonies to the power of the Gospel, and who like Stephen of old are full of the Holy Ghost and of power, are most likely to be successful in overcoming the formidable antagonism of modern doubt.

While feeling this most deeply, we will endeavour to add a few remarks, which may be useful alike to him who seeks to help the doubter and to the doubter himself.

First, Let us bear in mind *the probability of there being a moral cause at the root of our intellectual unbelief,* even though it be a *latent* cause. He who studies his own heart will be aware how subtle are the workings of pride; and one not uncommon form of this evil consists in a disposition to demand information in regions where it is necessarily beyond our reach, and to reject testimony which bears upon its surface the marks of apparent improbability. We are not born doubters, but are baptized in our early years into the Christian Church, and trained in childhood in Christian doctrine. It may well be demanded then, Did

we, when doubts first assailed us, humble ourselves to seek guidance from a God whom we
then professed to believe in, and obtain help from
others, whose judgment we were bound to respect,
upon our difficulties, as one after another they
arose? Too often the doubter gets into a state
of intellectual *flurry* and bewilderment, like a bird
beating against the bars of its cage, as "one
trouble calls another on," and one difficulty suggests another, and thus the edifice of faith falls
by-and-by with a crash, having been undermined
simultaneously all round, whereas if one doubt
had been calmly faced at a time, many would
have subsided altogether, and others might have
ceased to cause grave distress, even though the
question remained unsolved.

We must also remember that it is very difficult
to divest our mind of a certain feeling of superiority
to the many when we begin to harbour doubts.
The thoughtless many are ever credulous, and
prone to believe in marvels and prodigies, in
ghost-stories and apparitions; the thoughtful few
are indisposed to give credence to the supernatural
and inclined to be suspicious of even strong *primâ
facie* evidence in its favour. How often does a
secret prejudice against the probability of the

supernatural lie at the root of much of our modern
unbelief! A great point is gained when men see
that, granted a moral purpose in the universe, the
supernatural becomes at once *à priori* probable;
for how otherwise should God reveal Himself *as a
Person* to those who find in the regularity of nature
only the demonstration of the presence of a power
or a law?

Our next suggestion shall be, *Let us, in endeavouring to combat doubt, whether in ourselves or others,
begin by seeking to make sure of our foundation.*
We are persuaded that a great mistake is made
when we begin by endeavouring to establish such
subsidiary points as the inspiration or even general
authenticity of the canon of Holy Scripture; it was
not here that the Apostles of old sought to lay their
foundation in assailing an unbelieving or misbe-
lieving world. They preached JESUS, and upon
this tried stone once laid proceeded to raise the
structure of systematic doctrine. There is something in the character of the God-man so altogether
unique, that when He is lifted up, He draws all
men to Him still, and the wandering sons of men
still find in Him the way to the Father. In the
acceptance of the historical Christ, something like
a common basis is established between the doubter

and him who seeks to help him; and when the admission, "Surely this man was the Son of God," can be obtained, other important truths and doctrines will follow in due course; but this must come first.

Once again, we would suggest a *fearless appeal to the moral and religious instincts of the human heart.* This may be done by an exposure of the insufficiency of the utilitarian hypothesis to account for the phenomena of conscience, and to explain the inward pain caused by sin, or it may be done by pointing out the incongruity between man's recognized desires and aspirations and the conditions of his present existence. To the unbeliever life must needs appear as one grim tragedy from beginning to end; he is the victim of his own greatness, and may well envy his dog. On the other hand, he who has found his rest in Christ is conscious of a satisfaction, a peace, and a calm which exactly corresponds with his own heart's desires. There is a certain yearning after the infinite and the permanent in man, which is, we may say, set at defiance by all the conditions of his material existence, while on the other hand it is recognised and responded to by Revelation. We have seldom. if ever, seen this argument stated

as forcibly as it might be, but we are persuaded
it is a most cogent one ; its major premiss is to
be found in the fact there is *in nature* a certain
correspondency and relative fitness between the
various sentient objects in the world and the conditions with which they are surrounded. The fish
is so organised as to be comfortable and free from
pain in its native element, while to a creature
differently organised chronic immersion would be
torture, and so with all the other grades of the
animal kingdom ; is it reasonable to suppose that
man, incomparably her grandest work, is Nature's
one chosen victim, cursed with an elevation which
renders him incapable of satisfaction with the
condition of his existence, and exposed to grievous
sufferings and apprehensions from which other less
highly organised beings are exempt? To accept
such a position is surely to impugn the consistency
of nature, and this we shall not be led to do by
the careful study of her laws.

Two more suggestions we will hazard ere we take
leave of the subject of objective doubt, and the
first shall be that much help may be often obtained
*by contemplating as at a glance the various convergent
lines of evidence which lead up to the conclusion that
Christianity is the Truth.* It has often been found

helpful to set before the very eyes of a doubting inquirer some simple but forcible representation of the strength of the position which we maintain in this respect.   We would even venture to suggest some such device as the following to bring the thought the more powerfully before the apprehen-

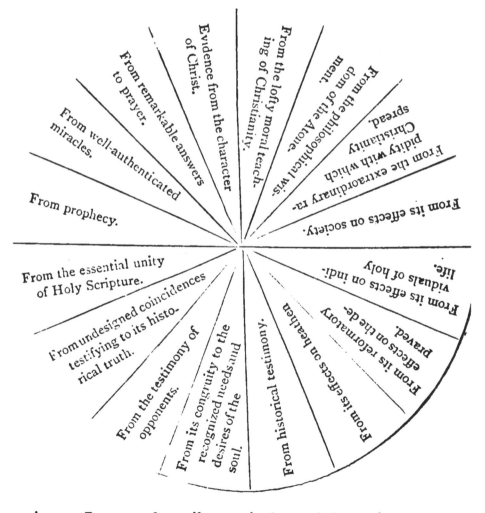

sion.   Let us describe a circle and from its centre draw a considerable number of radiating lines to the circumference, and into each of the spaces thus enclosed introduce the title of some distinct branch of Christian evidence.

Many other lines will suggest themselves probably to thoughtful minds, but the benefit of this method is that it presents us at a glance with a good idea of the weight of evidence that may be brought to bear. Perhaps no one of these lines of evidence in itself would be sufficient to establish the claims of a religious system upon our confidence, but each one of them will carry considerable weight with an honest inquirer, and surely the cumulative force of all put together is irresistible ; how many a man's life has paid forfeit to the law on evidence not nearly so strong and convincing !

Our last suggestion shall be, *that even when all else fails, prayer may prevail,* believing prayer on the part of the helper, *hypothetical prayer,* if needs be, on the part of the helped.

Who shall say that God would turn away from the prayer of Frederick's dying grenadier, "O God, if there be a God, save my soul, if I have a soul"? If we can go no further than this, it is surely worth while to throw all the energies of our soul into such an agonizing cry ; for are we not praying against corruption and darkness and destruction from the things that be? and is there not on the other side the splendid possibility of honour, glory, immortality, eternal life?

# CHAPTER V.

## INTELLECTUAL DIFFICULTIES ARISING FROM CERTAIN RELIGIOUS THEORIES.

NEXT in order to the difficulties arising from objective unbelief come those which are attributable to intellectual misapprehension of revealed truth. In many cases, no doubt, *peculiar religious views* are assumed as a sort of refuge of lies, behind which those who have no wish to be disturbed may more conveniently entrench themselves, and flatter their hearts with the cry, "Peace, peace, when there is no peace." But it is not with such that we have to deal in these papers; we have to confine ourselves to the consideration of the difficulties and perplexities of the honest and earnest seeker after God and His salvation; and it is only too evident that persons belonging to this class are not unfrequently impeded by cherished doctrines and theories in their attempts to obtain what in their hearts they feel they need.

Instances of this kind are supplied in connection

with the teaching of each of the three great schools of thought which are prominent within our Church at the present moment, and this fact renders it all the more difficult to deal with this part of our subject. Nothing is further from the object of these pages than doctrinal controversy, yet is it scarcely possible to clear the ground at this point without speaking plainly, and even strongly, upon subjects which both in our own and other ages have given occasion to much theological disputation. We hope it is possible to touch upon controverted points in an uncontroversial spirit, the more so as our object is to meet practical difficulties, and not to discuss abstract theological theories. For it must often have occurred to us all to observe how nearly really earnest and spiritually-minded men approach each other in practice, though their theories may appear to differ widely; and as it is with practice that we have to do here, I may venture to hope that I shall not incur the reputation of a spiritual Ishmaelite, if I refer with freedom to certain actual, though perhaps not always necessary, effects of the teaching of each of the prominent parties in our Church upon some to whom we would fain hold out a helping hand.

A very considerable number of awakened souls, of whose earnestness and desire to do what is right there can be small doubt, are kept back from enjoying the full privileges of the spiritual life by doubts on the Atonement. Such persons delight in contemplating the moral aspects of our Blessed Lord's Passion to which the Broad Church party so ably and eloquently witnesses, but they shrink sometimes with undisguised aversion from any doctrine of expiation or substitution, and plead that it is surely possible for God to forgive us just because He is a Father, and without any reference to the vicarious sufferings of another. It would probably be alleged by some, that difficulties of this class are not, properly speaking, difficulties of the soul at all, but difficulties created by the theologian; that they only are responsible for the existence of these difficulties who block up the way home to the Father's house with the insuperable barriers of a cumbrous Pauline Evangelicism; and that the easy way to meet such difficulties is to sweep these barriers on one side, and bid the soul pass on.

To such a position we have to reply, first, that we are expressly contemplating the case (and it is not a rare one) of those who by their own sorrowful admission have not succeeded in finding apart from the Atonement that inward experience which the New Testament so distinctly delineates, and which their own hearts long for, and who yet shrink from the mode of access to it which the New Testament prescribes, because it seems opposed to their moral sense. And next, our sense of duty to souls compels us to add the expression of our grave apprehension that too many of those who stumble at the Atonement without making any such admission, are themselves equally devoid of true spiritual experience in their religion. It is, however, specially with the former class that we have to do, and to them we would point out that the Atonement is indeed a mystery, but need not be a difficulty; indeed, that it is the only way out of a great and obvious difficulty.

Have those who find a difficulty in the orthodox view of the Atonement ever reflected on the graver moral difficulties which beset a theory of universal pardon? How impossible the schoolmaster, the employer, the ruler, often find it to exercise the prerogative mercy even in cases where it may appear that repentance is deep and genuine! Have those who would dispense with the Atonement faced the not improbable contingency that the reign of unqualified mercy might corrupt a universe of worlds? The point that those need to have made plain who are really seeking for peace, and would fain find it in truth revealed, but are repelled by the theory of the Atonement, is surely this, that God stands in a double relation to us His creatures. He is our Father, for we are all His offspring, but He is also our Sovereign, and as such the vindicator of His own laws. In that He is our Father, His reception of the sinner is an act of personal and unqualified forgiveness, and therefore there is nothing said about satisfaction in such passages as the parable of the prodigal son. In that He is the Ruler of the universe, however, and the Judge of all, His reception of the sinner is a judicial act of justification, and one that is only possible when in some way or other the great ends of justice have been answered, the sanctity of law vindicated, and the repetition and imitation of the offence rendered at least as improbable as if the merited punishment had actually been endured by the offender.

But these are precisely the effects which the Atonement is designed to induce, and as a matt.r of fact does produce, in the lives of thousands year by year. No man can be in a position to derive comfort from the Atonement, who does not intelligently contemplate the Cross, and apprehend, in some degree at any rate, the great lessons which are so conspicuous there. Unqualified forgiveness extended to the sinner could scarcely fail to suggest to his heart the thought, that God cannot feel strongly about the sin that He forgives so readily. The Cross of Calvary exhibits the most startling and convincing of all demonstrations of God's inexorable antipathy to, and necessary condemnation of, sin. Unqualified forgiveness leaves the moral character of the sinner just what it was before. Pardon through the Cross separates between the sinner and his former sins, and presses on his heart the thought, "How shall we who are dead to sin live any longer therein?" Thus so far from the doctrine of a vicarious atonement being, as it is sometimes called, a demoralizing figment, it is, on the contrary, the express provision of the Sovereign Judge of all to prevent pardon from being demoralizing.

We are persuaded that the mere indication of this double relationship in which God stands to man will, in a large number of cases where the soul is really seeking for light, be enough to clear away what is to many a very grave an ¹ serious difficulty.

One or two other thoughts suggest themselves to our mind ere we pass on from this subject.

First, It is well for those whose minds are exercised with doubts as to the justice of a vicarious atonement to bear in mind the eternal Divinity of the Sin-bearer, and His essential unity with His Father. It is this only that renders substitution either righteous or possible. Next, it is well to remember that while in His humanity as the sufferer He was called to endure what none but Himself could have endured, so He received a compensatory reward, the grandest and noblest that can be conceived—the right, as Man and in His Name of *Jesus,* to claim mercy for, and extend pardon to, a ransomed world, so that even in His human and personal experience, in spite of His cruel and overwhelming sufferings, He has gained, not lost, by His voluntary vindication of the majesty of His Father's law.

And once again, they whose difficulties assume this form need to have it clearly set before them that there is a great difference between understanding or even accepting any definite view or theory of the Atonement, and resting the soul on the fact. Our intellectual apprehension may reach no further than this, that whatever barrier may have existed, by the righteous judgment of God against sin, between us and Divine mercy, has been removed by the death of Christ; and yet we may with simple and heartfelt confidence trust ourselves to Him, persuaded that He has done all things that were needful for us, and in that trust find the assurance of pardon and peace. Fuller light on the mysteries of the Atonement may come by-and-by to render our confidence more intelligent and therefore more soul-satisfying, but for our personal security surely this rest in the Person of Christ is enough.

Another kind of difficulty which has not unfrequently to be encountered by the seeking soul arises from a sincere and conscientious desire duly to honour and value a sacred ordinance ordained by Christ Himself, and evidently designed to occupy a position of great prominence in the economy of the Christian Dispensation. The inquirer feels that in his inmost experience he needs something he has not yet obtained; he is uneasy and far from happy; he hears it strongly stated by the Evangelist that pardon, and reconciliation to God, and the authority to become a son of God, are all dependent on faith in Christ Jesus. He further hears a new life described as springing from this—a life of love, of liberty, and power. His own heart tells him that such are not the characteristics of his own experience; but if he accepts the preacher's assertions, which certainly seem to be supported by certain passages of Holy Scripture, what becomes of Holy Baptism and of all the spiritual blessings of which he believes he was made the unconscious recipient in his infant days?

Here again our desire is to deal practically, and not controversially, with a matter upon which so many differences of opinion exist; and without entering upon any elaborate disquisition on the subject of what is the true and what the false doctrine of Baptismal Regeneration, it will be enough, probably, if we take the honest seeker after truth, whose difficulties are of this order, to begin with on his own ground, by referring him to his Prayer Book, and above all to his Catechism. Here we have it distinctly laid down, that repentance and faith are required of all adults before Baptism can be administered: the obvious inference is suggested, that no Baptism administered without the presence of these conditions can be of any spiritual benefit to the recipient. We are further instructed that these are promised on be-half of the infant, and that this promise he himself

is bound to perform on coming to years of dis-
cretion. But surely here the inference is equally
strong and irresistible, that if the conditions be not
complied with, the provisional benefit, whatever it
may have been, must needs be forfeited.

It remains then, for such an one as we have
described, if he feels uneasy as to his spiritual
condition, to ask himself whether he has been
conscious of that "repentance whereby we forsake
sin," and of that "faith whereby we stedfastly
believe the promises of God made to us in that
sacrament." In this last remarkable expression,
let it be observed, the ordinance is represented as
the expression of God's promises towards us; and
when we ask for an explanation of the phrase, we
find it in the Article—"The promises of the forgiveness of sin, and of our adoption to be the sons
of God by the Holy Ghost, are visibly signed and
sealed." Has the inquiring soul ever claimed with
stedfast faith the fulfilment of these promises?
Has he trusted himself to Christ in order to realize
that of which Holy Baptism is at once the symbol
and the pledge? The ordinance itself is not only
a promise; it is a promise *because* it is the symbolic
representation of *a fact*—death unto sin, new life
unto God. I can therefore stedfastly believe the

promise only as my faith apprehends the fact, as I see myself represented in Christ in His death, and form the judgment which St. Paul formed long ago—"If one died for all, then all died." It will be seen that by insisting on these conditions we cast no slight on Holy Baptism, but rather urge that due heed shall be given to its clear and forcible teaching, and that it shall be accepted as the seal of a promise which God fulfils to us the moment that we comply with the appointed conditions.

Once again, it sometimes happens that the perplexities of seeking souls arise from their brooding over the mysterious subject of Divine foreknowledge and predestination. This is not a fancied but a very real source of difficulty. How often does it fall to the lot of a helper in a mission to meet with persons who are apparently very miserable and wretched, and would fain be altogether different from what they are, but who are kept back by the firm persuasion that there is nothing for it but to wait God's time. When the day of His power comes, they will be made willing; till then it is vain to pray, for what profit is there in a dead soul's prayers? how can they reach a living God who requires to be worshipped

in spirit and in truth ?   Impossible to repent, for
God must give repentance!   Impossible to believe,
for God must give faith !   If God intends them
to be saved, they will be saved ; and if they are
" vessels of wrath," they will be damned, do what
they will.   However startling such language may
sound to those whose Calvinism is of the modified
type common amongst Evangelical Christians, we
can assure our readers that we have done nothing
more than state these difficulties in the way in
which we have heard them stated over and over
again in conversations with anxious souls.

Now whatever mysteries may environ this subject of Divine election, arising as they probably do
out of the necessary relations of time to eternity,
and of the Absolute to the conditioned, one thing
is sufficiently plain, if we are to be guided by Holy
Scripture, namely, that God expects us to act in
response to His call, whether it comes directly or
indirectly, and never instructs us to wait till we
are acted on by a power that we cannot resist.
Ten times in New Testament Scripture the word
" repent " is uttered as a command in the impera-
tive mood, not once is the awakened sinner taught
to wait for repentance.   And not less frequently
is the word used in such a connection as to imply

that to decline to repent is a great and terrible
sin, meriting and bringing down upon the heads
of those who commit it God's condign punishment. If we are unable to obey a divinely given
direction of a positive character, we must needs,
by parity of reasoning, be incapable of complying
with a negative prohibition. He then who pleads,
" I cannot repent until God makes me," must be
fully prepared to accept the excuse of the pick-
pocket who robs him of his watch—"I cannot
leave off stealing till God constrains me to do so."

What such people have to learn is, that God
gives indirect as well as direct calls, and that the
Word of God read or heard or pressed home by
the entreaties of an earnest Christian is such an
indirect call, and that unless he acts upon it, and
turns from his sins, and flies to God for salvation,
he is as surely resisting the Holy Ghost as ever
did the murderers of Stephen. They need to
learn that the faintest desire after better things,
the inward thirst, the conviction of sin, the sense
of misery and wretchedness, are in themselves so
many signs of the Holy Spirit's influence, at work
within their hearts. And such lingerers need
sometimes to be reminded with tender severity
that it is possible for us, as did the Jews, to form

a preconceived idea of what our day of visitation is to be, while all the time we are wasting the day of visitation that God has actually given us. The charge against Jerusalem was not that she had consciously sinned away, but that *she knew not* the day of her visitation: is there not a danger of our doing the same while we wait on through long and wasted years for some extraordinary and supernatural manifestation which shall render us no longer masters of our own actions, and convert us into machines, in order to make us saints?

These are by no means the only forms, we need hardly remark, that theological difficulties may assume when they stand between the soul and Christ, but they may serve as specimens of others; and what is true of them will apply to other forms that may suggest themselves to our mind. Theological truth, when it comes between the soul and Christ, becomes a weapon in the hand of the father of lies, and is scarcely less dangerous than theological falsehood. The first, though not by any means the only office of theological truth, is to reveal to the wandering children of men the reconciled Father through the Son; and when we insist on employing her first on other matters instead of this, we must not complain of our guidē, if she lead into the chamber of mystery, instead of into the City of Vision; and we have ourselves to thank for it, if we measure out a dreary existence in wandering about in the profound depths and gloomy recesses of that hidden chamber, starving upon the unsubstantial fruit of the tree of knowledge while we turn our backs upon the Tree of Life.

> Where have ye laid Him? in what tomb
>   Of ancient creed or modern doubt,
> In depths of philosophic gloom,
>   Close wrapt with 'wildering words about?
> Give me my Lord! to soothe, to save,
> Or I sink deeper than the grave.
>
> Give me my Lord! your subtle thoughts
>   But mock the hunger of the soul ·
> I turn from all your lore hath brought—
>   Give me my Lord, to make me whole,
> To calm my fears, my guilt remove :
> Give me my Lord, for *He is Love.*   JOHN xx. 15.

# CHAPTER VI.

## THE USUAL ORDER OF EVENTS IN THE SOUL'S EXPERIENCE.

THE difficulties which we have hitherto been considering have been those which affect the mind rather than the heart. We proceed now to deal with those which concern the heart rather than the mind. We will only pause to point out, in passing, that the line of distinction between intellectual and moral or spiritual difficulties cannot be as sharply and as accurately defined as might at first sight appear; for who shall say how large a proportion of the intellectual error which blinds our vision and arrests our approach to God is due to moral or spiritual causes? and who shall say how much of our moral or spiritual perplexity and bewilderment arises from intellectual ignorance and confusion? The truth is, that, in spite of the complexity of his nature, man is one, and whatever affects, whether injuriously

5

or otherwise, any one element of his nature, to a greater or less extent affects all.

To this close connection between the mind and the moral nature of man are to be attributed those ancient philosophic speculations which identified virtue with knowledge and vice with ignorance, a theory which, though we may not be disposed wholly to accept it, must be admitted to contain a very considerable amount of truth. Thus far experience constrains us to go, that there are few forms of moral evil that do not either spring from, or are justified, extenuated, or excused by, a perverted understanding ; and that no man can lead a life of habitual sin, without his understanding becoming so *practically* darkened, and his powers of discernment so dulled, that he will not only call " evil good and good evil," but " the bitter sweet and the sweet bitter."

It will therefore fall to our lot, in pursuing our subject, still to deal largely with errors and misconceptions of the understanding, even while we are following the soul through those passages in its experience in which, above all others, the emotions and the will have such an important part to play, and are necessarily so strongly affected. We shall perhaps be in a better position to deal with difficulties of both kinds, and to map out our subject in a clear and methodical manner, if we begin by giving as succinctly as possible a general sketch of what would seem to be the usual —perhaps we may say the normal—course of God's dealings with the human soul, and of its experiences, in a true conversion. Only, let us be careful to remind our readers, as we attempt to do so, that God is bound by no stereotyped form of procedure, and that His modes of dealing with our souls are as various as the dispositions with which He has to deal. All that we propose to do is to indicate the usual, not the invariable or universal, order of events in this important epoch in spiritual experience.

This, at least, we may lay down as certain and invariable, that the gracious influences of the Holy Spirit must first be brought to bear upon the heart of man before he will be disposed to turn from sin and seek pardon and peace. Unless His grace prevent us, no action of ours can lead to a satisfactory issue. Here, however, we have no grounds for apprehension: dependent though we needs must be upon Him, we need not fear that any of us will ever have occasion to blame Him for failing in His part. We may be very sure that the Holy Spirit, who has affirmed "All souls are mine," is at least as assiduous in His efforts to influence the souls of men for God and for good, as the spirit of evil is to tempt and mislead; but men need to be solemnly warned that His influence may not unfrequently be brought to bear upon us indirectly, so that we may not recognise it as coming from Him, and yet be none the less such a call as, if responded to, would have brought us at once within reach of salvation. Now, when the Holy Spirit strives with us, whether directly or indirectly, one of two courses is open to us— either we may harden our hearts against Him, as we are expressly warned not to do, or we may yield ourselves to His influence, and surrender to His summons. If we adopt the former of these courses, we sink into a more profound spiritual slumber than if we had never been roused at all; while, on the other hand, if we yield, the result will be *spiritual awakening.*

"He came to himself:" this was the turning-point in the history of the prodigal son, that marvellous picture of a true repentance drawn by the Master's hand, and it is the turning-point in most cases still. The soul becomes fully conscious of its folly, its danger, and its needs, and begins to ask with ever deepening interest, What must I do to be saved? The first motives of the awakened soul are by no means the purest or the most exalted; indeed, it is often a matter of complaint with such, that they seem to be actuated only by a selfish and servile desire to escape hell, or to be relieved from present suffering. Upon this difficulty we must touch more fully by-and-by. For the present it may suffice that we remind our readers of the distinction so well drawn by Butler between selfishness and rational self-love. The instinct of self-preservation, so strong in us all, extends to the region of moral and spiritual action, and doubtless has been implanted in order that it may be employed for the best purposes by Him who implanted it. God takes us where He finds us, that He may bring us whither He would have us brought.

At this point it will doubtless be recorded of the troubled and agitated soul, as it was of one of old, "Behold, he prayeth,"—prayeth as one in desperate circumstances, overwhelmed with a consciousness of need, oftentimes pouring forth "strong cries and tears," as though he would take heaven by storm; at other times benumbed and paralysed by a sense of moral helplessness, only able to smite on his breast, and cry, "God be merciful to me a sinner."

It is when the light has thus entered the soul, revealing to us our true condition, that the Spirit of God leads us up to the point of *definite decision* which is usually the next step in the soul's experience. Let it not be thought that this is necessarily implied in what we have already described. A man may be aroused, alarmed, even distressed, and yet he may not finally decide at all costs to turn his back on sin and yield himself to God; and when the soul halts and hesitates at this point, the spiritual agitation to which I have referred soon begins to subside, the hurt is healed over slightly, and the heart becomes harder than ever before. After he had come to himself, the prodigal had still to say, "I will," and all is lost when this point is not gained.

At this crisis it is that the soul will probably be constrained deliberately to "count the cost," and to consider whether he is prepared to sacrifice all that seems to come between him and his God, and here often a terrible struggle takes place ere he is able to exclaim, "My heart is fixed, O God, my heart is fixed." It is usually after this decision has been made, and when the mind, no longer preoccupied with a terrible struggle, is as it were given up to the influences of the Holy Spirit, that a deep and humbling *conviction of sin* is felt. Here again the parable of the prodigal son casts its clear light on our subject. The decision was first arrived at, " I will arise and go to my father," and then it is that with the very expression of the decision, there rises in his mind the recollection of the foul wrong that he has done that father, the thought of his unworthiness again to enjoy that father's society, and his recognition of the degradation and disgrace that he has richly merited.

How often has it fallen to our lot to witness similar experiences ! The moment that the decision was reached, it has seemed as if "all the fountains of the great deep " within were indeed "broken up;" often the reluctant tears have at last begun to flow, or even where these were absent a consciousness of God's love and our ingratitude has produced a sense of penitential sorrow, often more precious in God's sight than even tears. Or sometimes it happens that in phlegmatic and unemotional temperaments the same state of soul will be indicated by a certain impatience at ourselves because we don't feel the sorrow that we wish to feel; and who shall say that the honest wish to feel is less acceptable than the feeling in the eyes of Him "who knoweth our frame"?

In whatever form, however, our sense of sin may find expression, it will be there; and as we acknowledge the truth of the charges brought against us by the Holy Spirit, we shall be brought to the next step, which will be usually *confession and humiliation*. It has to be borne in mind that true repentance is essentially personal; it does not consist in feeling so much sorrow or in shedding so many tears, but in taking our true place in the dust at the feet of Him whom we have sinned against, and acknowledging our offence.

It is when we thus approach God, that the thought of our unfitness to draw near to Him becomes so overwhelming, that we are, as it were, constrained to look out of ourselves for a plea, and thus it is that we are brought to the point of *apprehension*, when the eye of faith is at length fixed upon Him whom God has provided to meet our case. It often happens that the Cross of Christ seems little better than a strange enigma, when first the soul turns its wearied, longing gaze towards it. We fail at first clearly to discern its bearings on our case; by-and-by, whether we understand all that it means or not, we begin to reflect that it is surely specially designed by God Himself to meet our wants, and that therefore all that we require must be there. Then our vision clears, and we discern our old man crucified together with Christ, that the body of sin might be destroyed.

Thus we are led on to the final step, of *simple trust in a personal Saviour for present salvation;* and no sooner is this attitude of the soul towards Him assumed, than we find ourselves entitled to grasp and appropriate to ourselves all the benefits of the Atonement. Then its blessed assurance of immunity from condemnation and security from danger begins at once to produce its necessary effect upon the emotions; fear becomes impossible where its causes are eliminated; the inward tumult of conflicting feelings ceases as there steals over the soul a blessed sense of rest and peace, accompanied in some instances by a joy that is indeed "unspeakable and full of glory." Thus the believing soul enters upon the *full assurance of present salvation,* and starts upon its course a new creature in Christ Jesus, still exposed to temptations, and liable to failure, but the slave of sin

and victim of the devil no longer; entitled, indeed.
to regard himself as "dead indeed unto sin, and
alive unto God through Jesus Christ our Lord."

In thus representing Conversion as a sort of
spiritual process with marked and definite stages,
the last thing that we desire is to give the impression that there is something very elaborate and
complicated in this passage from death unto life ;
nor would we lead any to suppose that a considerable time must necessarily be spent in passing
through these various experiences.   We wish this
description rather to be regarded as an analysis
of the most important event that can transpire in
any human life, and an arrangement of its constituent elements, so to speak, in their most usual
order of sequence.   As to its duration, the whole
event sometimes occupies only a few short hours,
and cases sometimes come under notice where a
change as radical and permanent as could be
desired is wrought almost in a moment, and
apparently without any such preparation as might
have been deemed necessary.   Our object is not
to complicate but to simplify matters, by endeavouring to clear the subject from the obscurity
which arises from vague and indefinite fancies
and an unintelligent assumption of mystery.

But chiefly we have offered this sketch of the steps by which we usually approach the Cross, because experience teaches us that at each of the stages to which we have referred, difficulties are apt to arise, and we are anxious that, as far as possible, none should escape our notice. To be forewarned is to be in some measure forearmed; and it is well that the seeking soul should be prepared to meet the enemy at the points where observation shows us the attack is most likely to be made.

Around the Cross of Christ we may say, to put the case in a somewhat allegorical form, the great enemy of mankind has contrived to construct a sort of labyrinth or maze of devious and bewildering paths, right through the midst of which there runs the strait and narrow way that leads directly to the Cross; but, by reason of the darkness which hovers round, and of the roughness of the ascent, the eye does not readily detect it. The soul has scarcely started on its progress toward the Cross before it finds itself accosted by the deceiver, not unfrequently in the garb of an angel of light; and if it listens to his suggestions, it may wear out a fruitless life in vain attempts to get nearer to the desired object, while really its energies are being wasted in going round and round it, becoming the while more and more hopelessly involved in the network of error. With each step forward a fresh risk is incurred; the first by-path is avoided, and perhaps the second; but just when the inquirer is flattering himself that the danger is over, a still more insidious suggestion takes him unawares, and before he has detected his error he finds himself involved in bewilderment and embarrassment, wandering further and further from peace and safety.

If then we can succeed in setting a few finger-posts, as it were, at those points on the King's highway where the false turn is most frequently taken, we shall not have wasted time in our attempt roughly to map out that highway itself, so far as we are permitted to know anything about it. And here, as our desire is to deal with the concrete rather than the abstract, with difficulties in the form which they practically assume, rather than with general hypotheses, it may be expedient to state these difficulties just in the terms in which they are frequently expressed by inquiring souls, and then to offer such answers and counsels as we are able.

I propose to commence the systematic treatment

of the various points thus suggested in the next chapter. Meanwhile let me earnestly call the attention of those who seek to help the soul in its passage through these experiences, to the importance of endeavouring as far as possible to find out what stage has actually been reached by those with whom they deal, and of determining their mode of action accordingly. An old proverb teaches us that " what is one man's meat is another man's poison," and a similar aphorism might well be laid down with respect to spiritual things— " What is needful for one is positively injurious to another." If, for example, an inexperienced helper begins by preaching faith to a half-awakened inquirer, he will probably only waste his breath or elicit the assertion that the person addressed has always "trusted the Almighty." Probably such treatment will only deepen the subtle self-complacency of one who above everything else needs to be thoroughly broken down, stript of his stolid equanimity, and led to see the plague of his own heart. On the other hand, if he attempt to deepen contrition in one who is already despondent, he is in danger of breaking a bruised reed, or of quenching the smoking flax.

Our true wisdom lies in endeavouring to co-operate with the Holy Spirit. We must needs be "workers together with Him," if we would be really successful in spiritual labour; but to do this we must find out what the Holy Spirit is teaching the soul, and endeavour to deepen that particular lesson ; or if that seems already well learned, we should conclude that He is leading on to the next step, and that He may intend to use us here.

In medicine, an accurate diagnosis is the first step towards a cure ; and with dealing with sin-sick souls, our ability to give real help must greatly depend on our apprehension of their real condition. Such wisdom cometh from Above, but he who would win souls must have it ; and is it not specially promised,—" If any man lack wisdom, let him ask of God, who giveth to all men liberally, and upbraideth not; and it shall be given him"?

# CHAPTER VII.

## DIFFICULTIES OF A MORAL OR SPIRITUAL KIND.

IN the sketch which our last chapter contained of the usual course of spiritual experience in a true repentance and conversion, it will be remembered that we indicated certain definite steps or stages through which souls most frequently pass very much in the order in which we arranged them. Now at each of these steps we are liable to be brought face to face with the difficulties, or to be perplexed or misled by the eriors, which specially beset that particular point in spiritual experience, but not all of us equally at every point. Some will be in special danger of being ensnared at the very outset, and of having all promise of real repentance nipped in the bud, while others may find the gravest conflict awaiting them at the very last step. When the chief difficulty will occur, must probably depend a good deal upon our natural temperament, our religious training, the clearness of the doctrinal teaching that we have received, the circumstances under which our impressions have been caused, and the depth and character of those impressions.

But as we would fain help all, we will take these possible difficulties and dangers in the order in which they may naturally be expected to occur, if the usual course of spiritual experiences be as we have described it. Our desire is to deal with these difficulties and errors in as concrete a form as possible, to present them to our readers in the most familiar guise, and then to endeavour to deal with them in as practical a way as we can. To effect this object, it occurs to us that we cannot do better than introduce these points by quoting phrases with which, on the lips of those whom we seek to help, we are only too familiar, and which we may regard as representing the objections or difficulties which occur in a large number of instances at particular points in spiritual experience.

We will begin with those which belong to the very earliest stages of religious awakening, and then proceed in the order which we have already laid down. These phrases shall form our texts, and we will then proceed to comment upon them ; and here is our first—

"*It is true I am a sinner, but I do not see that I am so very bad after all.*"

We are supposing these words to fall from the lips, not of an altogether self-complacent Pharisee (such cannot be regarded as even inquiring souls), but of one whose conscience is smarting with the pain of a secret wound, and who yet scarcely likes to admit that this is really the case ; the man who is making a last desperate effort to find something in himself to rest in, not because he is self-satisfied, but because he is extremely uncomfortable. To him who is held at this point we would suggest a few wholesome subjects for reflection ; and if he desires not to resist, but to co-operate with the Divine Spirit, he will find it helpful to ponder them well.

First, let him consider what it is that makes sin so exceedingly sinful. The sinfulness of sin will always bear an exact proportion to the privileges and advantages of the sinner. He sins most who sins against the clearest light and the most favourable circumstances. Next, let him remember that man's estimate of sin is not always the same as God's,—that sins that man may think lightly of, such as worldliness, covetousness, avarice, temper, and pride, are as surely sins in the eyes of God as those particular offences which society, for its own sake, severely reprobates. The Word of God teaches

6

that the thought of wickedness is sin, that hatred is simply another form of murder, and that a lustful look is in God's sight adultery.

Once again, let him observe that in almost every case where judgment is described in New Testament Scripture, it is represented as following sins *of omission.* To ensure our condemnation in the eyes of Him who has called us into existence for His own glory, it is enough if it can be shown that we have "come short," as St. Paul says *all have,* "of the glory of God" (Rom. iii. 23). Let it be proved against any of us, as it was proved against Belshazzar of old, that "the God in whose hand thy breath is. and whose are all thy ways, thou hast not glorified," and that will suffice to cause a stern and irrevocable "Tekel" to be recorded against our name—we are weighed in the balance, and found wanting.

Above all, let him reflect that the sin of sins lies in despising and making light of God's wondrous provision for our salvation ; that to slight the gift offered at such a price is to dishonour the Giver ; that no greater insult can be offered to the love of the Father and the devotion of the Son of God, than is offered by him who passes by the Cross as though it were nothing to him. And lastly, let

him bear in mind, that of all perilous sins, none
is more full of spiritual danger than sin against
the Holy Ghost; and let him consider whether
his frequent resistance of a holy influence that has
drawn him towards the Cross of Christ has not
partaken of this nature. "How canst thou say, I
am not polluted, I have not gone after Baalim?
See thy way in the valley. *Know what thou hast
done*" (Jer. ii. 23).

"*It is no use for me to try to be good; I
am too bad ever to be a Christian.*"

In the contrast between these two cases we have
an illustration of the wondrous versatility which
characterizes the operations of the foe. This
sudden change of front has from remote antiquity
formed a feature of his too skilful tactics. We
have already quoted the expostulation of the
ancient seer against Israel's hypocritical self-complacency. Only a few lines further on we find
just such an utterance as the present put into the
mouth of the same nation: "But thou saidst,
There is no hope: no; for I have loved strangers,
and after them I will go."

It is, however, in some respects, a more hopeful
sign when we hear the awakened sinner using this
sort of language; at any rate, it usually argues that

the man is thoroughly out of conceit with himself, and has reached the point of self-despair ; and we cannot too emphatically state that until this point is reached there is no real ground for hope. There is, however, a serious danger here, which needs to be guarded against. Self-despair, if it does not lead to trust in the living God, will certainly generate recklessness, and this is precisely the evil of which the prophet has to complain in the passage that we have just quoted. To avoid this, he who is halting at this point needs to call to mind the old proverb, " Man's extremity is God's opportunity." If we have found out our utter inability to deliver ourselves, surely it is high time that we should inquire, in the language of the seventh of Romans, " *Who* will deliver me ? " If the work is to be done by man, it is indeed a hopeless task ; but if by God, with Him nothing is impossible.

Let such an one begin by forming a definite apprehension of what it is that the Gospel does, and what it is that the Gospel does not, call upon him to do. The Gospel does not demand that the sinner shall endeavour to improve himself and make himself better, until at length he is good enough to be received into Divine favour.

This were indeed to impose an impossible condition upon the offer of salvation; for "who can
bring a clean thing out of an unclean?" The
Gospel does demand that the sinner shall recognize to the utmost his own moral impotence, and
that then just because he is helpless, he shall
accept the full deliverance which Christ offers to
the spiritual captive as the result of His atonement.
Is it in very deed "a trustworthy saying, deserving
of universal acceptance, that Jesus Christ came into
the world to save sinners"? If it be, then it can be
no more reasonable to decline to come to Christ
because we are bad, than it would be to decline
to call in a physician because we are seriously
sick, or to refuse to grasp a life-belt because we
feel ourselves drowning. It cannot be too clearly
stated, that sin is only then an obstacle to our
approach to the Saviour, when we are unwilling
to part company with it. Otherwise the reasoning
of omnipotent mercy is still what it was of old ·
"Though your sins be as scarlet, they shall be
white as snow; though they be red like crimson,
they shall be as wool."

Let such an one also encourage himself by
remembering what the triumphs of grace have
been in every age and are still. His case is **no**

worse than that of hundreds of others who, like the woman of Samaria of old, or the fallen one who wept at Jesus' feet, or the dying felon who claimed a Saviour's mercy almost with his latest breath, have proved that grace is stronger than sin, and the Divine Saviour mightier than all the malignant enmity of hell.

It cannot be too clearly explained that we **do** not ask the awakened sinner to try and become good, and so gradually to grow into a Christian. We ask him to confess his own utter badness and his incapacity to make himself better; and we ask him to see, with simple childlike faith, that badness of his, or, as St. Paul would express it, his " old man," "crucified with Christ, that the body of sin might be destroyed; " so that, trusting himself to the work of Christ on his behalf, he may become " a new creature " in Christ Jesus, and find all the wealth of Divine power within his reach to enable him to walk in newness of life, freed by the law of the Spirit of life in Christ Jesus from the old law of sin and death. It is of no use for him to try to be good, but it is of every use to make himself over into the hands of the faithful Creator, that he may be created anew in righteousness and true (actual) holiness.

*"I would like to be different from what
I am, but I fear I am not really awakened."*

Here we have a very favourite device of the
enemy exposed by the statement of the difficulty.
We have already had occasion to point out that
the great deceiver knows how to adjust his mode
of operation to our characters, temperaments, and
circumstances. There are many cases in which
the awakening of the soul is accompanied by such
startling experiences, that such a suggestion will
be in a moment confuted by facts; but it is not
always so; and when those experiences are absent,
Satan eagerly takes advantage of their absence to
discourage the awakening soul in its first attempts
to feel after God. He who listens to such a
suggestion will soon conclude that, as God has
not done His part, it is of no avail for him to
endeavour to do his, and thus he will be in danger
of relapsing into something even more deadly than
his old indifference.

To such an one we might put the case thus:
What should we think of a consumptive patient
who declined to avail himself of the assistance of
a physician, not because his judgment was not
convinced of his terrible danger, but because he
failed vividly *to realize* its magnitude? If your

own mind is so far aware of your danger, as that a desire has been awakened, however faint, to escape it, be reasonable enough to act upon that desire. Overwhelming consternation is not a necessary part of true repentance; if God be leading you by gentler influences to seek for what you feel you want, you are sufficiently awakened to value what He is willing to bestow, not because you are in a state of desperate alarm, but because He loves you, and has made provision for your safety. Do you not observe how differently God dealt with different people in New Testament times? The Ethiopian eunuch was not struck to the ground by a miraculous power; Saul of Tarsus was. Of Lydia we do not hear that she passed through any violent agitation; the jailer in the same town did; and yet all these were equally the recipients of God's saving grace.

"*I am devoid of the true motive for repentance; I am simply moved by a selfish desire to escape hell.*"

This is a very common and a very plausible difficulty. When subjected to careful analysis, however, this apparently humble confession turns out to be only a subtle and insidious form, if not of self righteousness, at any rate of would-be self trust.

We may add that this is the latent cause of a very large proportion of the difficulties that spring up as we attempt to approach the Cross. If we can present no good works of our own to win God's favour, at any rate it is something if we are actuated by the highest and purest motives. Next to never committing sin at all, what better could we desire than that we should have the same keen hatred of sin, as sin, which characterizes the nature of God? and next to never grieving God at all, what better could we, or even God, desire than that we should be overwhelmed with penitential distress at the thought of ever having grieved Him? Surely, the deceitful heart argues, if we could only present this, it would be impossible for God to turn His back upon us; while, on the other hand, if we do not possess it, how can we hope for His favour?

Those who think or feel thus, under whatever approved and orthodox form of expression they conceal their thoughts or feelings, need to learn what those well-known lines mean, that probably they themselves so often sing,—

> "Nothing in my hand I bring,
>   Simply to Thy cross I cling."

Obviously they are deferring their approach to

Christ until they are conscious of having attained a certain form of experience which usually results from our having come to Him. They are waiting for the effect to produce the cause, instead of leaving the cause to produce the effect. They are practically " tarrying till they are better," instead of coming to Christ to make them what in themselves they are not. For surely this keen sensitiveness to sin, this overwhelming sense of its exceeding sinfulness, this tender contrition and sorrow towards God at the thought of ever having grieved Him, are for the most part, at any rate, the features of an advanced and fully developed spiritual experience, and certainly are not what we should look for from one who has not yet begun to know what spiritual experience is. We do not deny that God's Holy Spirit can, and sometimes does, produce these feelings in the heart of a newly awakened sinner, but surely that is no reason why all should expect them, and still less is it a reason why any should consider themselves precluded from all access to the Cross of Christ because such experiences are not theirs.

To all who have difficulties of this order we would point out that in redemption God comes to us *where we are,* and takes us as we are. He drives no bargain with us, demanding that we should first exhibit desirable moral or spiritual qualities, before we can become the recipients of His favour, but He begins by appealing to those instincts of our nature which we certainly do possess, and then leads us up higher. We need not rail against ourselves because our motives are selfish, but rather remember Butler's most reasonable distinction to which we have before referred between selfishness and natural self-regard. God Himself has furnished our nature with certain self-regarding instincts, and in acting upon these we are not exhibiting selfishness, but rational self-love.

An enlightened sense of self-interest was the first motive-power that induced the prodigal to return home. He does not seem to have been moved in the first instance by a deep sense of contrition at the thought of his conduct towards his father; it was rather that death evidently stared him in the face, and in his father's house lay the only door of hope.

" How many hired servants of my father's have bread enough and to spare, and I perish with want !" Here his repentance began, but not here did it end; the man that responds to these lower motives by saying, as the prodigal did say, "*I will*," must soon find himself face to face with God's love, and his abuse of it, and thus his motives will become almost unconsciously elevated and purified ; but in this case he will no longer be in danger of presenting these higher motives as a sort of purchase-money for Divine favour, seeing he is already beginning to enjoy the consciousness of God's favourable regard.

"*I have no real desire to come to Christ.*"

This is a particularly difficult objection to deal with, and it is one that, when once taken up, is frequently clung to with a pertinacity almost amounting to obstinacy.   The special difficulty is perhaps due to the fact that you can only meet it by combating its truth ; and it does seem little short of an impertinence to profess to know more of a person's inner experiences than he does himself.

Yet this is often the actual state of the case.   A common proverb affirms that "a looker-on knows most of the game ; " and it not unfrequently happens that the soul is so agitated by conflicting experiences, so bewildered by unaccustomed attempts at introspection, that it cannot admit the calm and dispassionate view of its own case that a Christian adviser or friend will naturally take. What does this startling assertion really mean?

If it be literally true, the case is foreclosed, and it is difficult to see what more can be done or said ; for without some kind of desire there can be no moral action ; but is it actually true ?   Is not the very fact that such words often—usually, indeed— are met with on the lips of an inquirer—of one, that is to say, who is content to submit to accept, or even to seek for, that which so many shrink from— spiritual counsel and assistance, a sufficient indication that, whatever may be asserted to the contrary, some kind of desire is present ?   Is not the person who so speaks generally uneasy, discontented, far from happy ?   The error which leads to such a depressing conclusion usually lies in the acceptance of some theory about *desire* which is wholly at variance with fact.

Frequently, if the question is put, "Would you not like to be a real Christian?" the answer is, "Oh, yes ! I should like to be, but then I have no real desire ; it is only that my judgment is persuaded that the Christian's life is the best, and I am not without apprehensions that a terrible doom may be in store for me, unless I turn to God." But what is this but a desire, albeit a very faint and imperfectly developed one?   There is a point in the nature of man where the desires and the reasoning or apprehending faculties meet, and, as it were, run into each other, so that it is not easy to predicate of a particular state of consciousness arising in this region, whether it should be regarded as a mental conviction or a moral desire. But little or nothing is gained by an elaborate psychological analysis of our inward experiences; we only perplex ourselves in our attempts to decide what is mental and what moral. The real point at issue is, am I or am I not aware of an inward need? if I am, that is enough to act upon.

When we approach a meal, we do not begin by asking ourselves whether we have an appetite; it is enough that reason has taught us that the body requires to be fed, and accordingly we proceed to feed it. Yet all the while an undeveloped desire is present within us, as is proved by the fact that the reception of food is agreeable and not distasteful to us. Would there be any wisdom in denying ourselves food until we have a ravenous appetite? surely it is still more unreasonable to deny our souls what they most need, because we have no very distinct consciousness of an inward desire. The voice of infinite mercy proclaims as truly now as in the temple of old, "If any man thirst, let him come unto Me, and drink." Observe, He does not say, If any man thirst for Me; we may not as yet feel any positive desire for God, yet may we be able to comply in a true, though somewhat negative, sense with the terms or condition of the invitation; we do thirst, that is to say, we are far from being satisfied; we are haunted with a sense of emptiness and want. It is enough; our David receives into his motley army "every one that is distressed, and every one that is in debt, and every one that is discontented" or "bitter of soul;" and as we draw near and cry to Him for salvation from the coldness of our spiritual insensibility, the genial influence of His love begins to awaken better and stronger desires, and to melt down the frigidity of our moral stupor, until at length we find ourselves breathing out our hearts with fervent longings: "My soul is athirst for God, yea, even for the living God;" and He satisfieth the longing soul, and filleth the hungry soul with goodness.

# CHAPTER VIII.

## DIFFICULTIES CONNECTED WITH FULL DECISION.

PURSUING the order of spiritual experiences which we sketched in a previous chapter, we come next to consider those difficulties which are connected with the full decision of the will. Here it is not unfrequently that the hardest battle has to be fought and the most serious obstacles overcome, and here too often the awakened soul looks back, ere yet the Zoar of safety is reached, and finds itself, like Lot's wife of old, the blighted victim of its own irresolution. Here, too, very often the task of the spiritual adviser is a most painful and even in appearance cruel one, as he finds himself constrained to point out the impossibility of making any kind of compromise between the claims of God and the seductions of the world and sin. Great is the need of wisdom as well as firmness in our endeavours to lead the awakened soul on to a full decision; for while on the one

**7**

hand we are bound in all honesty to encourage such to count the cost, and not to rush on in blind haste under the influence of excited enthusiasm, we need to be equally careful lest we quench a frail but sincere desire by too alarming a picture of possible consequences, or demand some definite step of agonizing self sacrifice, which may not perhaps after all be called for by the circumstances of the case.

Our difficulties in this respect are enhanced by the fact that it is so much easier for a man of the world to appreciate the losses than the gains of such a decisive step. He knows something about the attractions of the world and the pleasures of sin; he knows nothing as yet, except by hear-say, of the joys of a Christian's life, or of the present satisfaction of those who find their portion in their God. To such an one, therefore, it may seem as if we were asking him to stake his all on a venture, and possibly to forfeit the substance while he grasps at the shadow. On the other side, however, it should be remembered that an awakened soul has already begun to form a just estimate of the real, as distinct from the apparent, value of worldly things. He will have found out more or less fully by bitter experience their vapid inanity, and hence his better judgment is already on the side of that higher voice which bids him seek the things that are above. To refer again to that standard type of true repentance,—the parable of the prodigal son, the "mighty famine" and the conviction "I perish with want," led up to the decisive "I will," which was morally the first step of the homeward journey.

We will proceed to consider one by one the various obstacles that have to be surmounted ere we can truly say, "My heart is fixed, O God, my heart is fixed;" and foremost amongst these is *the love of some cherished sin.* It often happens that the spiritual guide, as he seeks to direct the feet of the wanderer into the way of peace, becomes aware of the presence of some invisible but very obvious obstruction. He makes no progress, the soul listens with ready attention to all that he can say; seems really awakened and distressed; and yet, no matter how plainly the truth of the Gospel is set before it, there seems to be a kind of moral incapacity to receive it in such a way as to derive any spiritual benefit from it. Then it becomes necessary for the skilful physician gently and tenderly to probe the wound, not in an inquisitive or censorious manner, but with all that delicate

sympathy which is required to elicit the soul's
deepest confidence. The question, " Is there anything between your soul and God ? " will often be
enough to bring to the surface the latent forces of
evil by which the soul is enthralled, sometimes in
a tacit admission, and sometimes in a definite
utterance. Here, however, it may be necessary to
remind our readers that sin is only in this sense of
the word *between* the sinner and his God when our
hearts still continue to cling to it, and are reluctant
to forsake it. It is not the heinousness nor **the**
frequency of our sins, but our unwillingness to be
saved from them, that creates a barrier between us
and God's free mercy in Jesus Christ.

When it is clearly discovered that some such
barrier does exist in the case of one whom we are
seeking to help, the question naturally arises, how
far have we a right to demand that the secret thing
shall be confessed to us ? how far is it possible for
us to be of real service to the awakened soul, if we
do not press such inquiries ? To this we reply
without hesitation, that experience teaches that in
a large number of cases it is a great help to a perplexed and bewildered soul, involved in the meshes
of some deadly sin, to disclose its inward snare
and hindrance to a wise and sympathetic friend,

who will be all the better able to help when he is acquainted in detail with the character of the difficulty. But on the other hand there are cases, in which no kind of uncertainty or perplexity exists, where little or nothing is gained by such a confession ; the statement of a general principle clearly covers the particular case, and all that is needed is to endeavour to induce decisive action of the will.

Inasmuch then as it must often be a doubtful point whether the statement of the evil will be a help towards its removal, our wisdom surely lies in leaving it to the judgment and feeling of the person whom we seek to help to decide whether or not the revelation of the secret obstacle will be a real assistance to its removal. No man surely has a right to thrust himself unbidden into the sacred solitude of another's inner life ; yet anxiety to give real help may justify us in craving admission thither if we feel persuaded that here our counsels and admonitions may be of good service.

It has been my practice in these pages not to shrink from all reference to controverted points, but to endeavour to touch upon them in an uncontroversial spirit ; and now that I find myself face to face with a subject upon which at the moment theological feeling on both sides is perhaps more sensitive than on any other, I must endeavour to pursue the same method. We so often hear it affirmed that the *"inquiry meeting"* is simply the confessional after a Protestant model, that we are constrained to point out wherein the two modes of dealing with the soul differ from each other ere we take leave of this part of the subject. The very term *"inquiry meeting"* indicates the cardinal distinction, suggesting as it does that this is a means designed to meet the inquiries of those who are in perplexities, and who seek help—not an inquisitorial rite designed to extract information as to the secret facts of our inward experience. In the one case confession is encouraged only for the sake of the increased facilities that it affords us of dealing with spiritual difficulties; in the other it is demanded first as an act of needful humiliation; second, as the condition of obtaining absolution and forgiveness. In the one case we only seek to become acquainted with such sin as the soul is clinging to, and leave those that it is willing to renounce to be confessed to God alone; in the other it matters not what our attitude to sin may be, the sins that we cling to and those that we fly from have alike to be spread out in all their perhaps loathsome detail before the spiritual director. In the one case the confession is the spontaneous act of the soul seeking to disburden itself of a load of perplexity and embarrassment as well as of guilt, and in the spontaneousness of the act lies its moral value, as thus the soul is laid open to all the helpful influence of Christian sympathy, whereas in the other case the confession is elicited by the exercise of ecclesiastical authority on the part of one who, as spiritual director, claims to be in possession of the secrets of the heart that he guides.  In the one case the soul voluntarily discloses the secret evil, because it feels that a certain sense of relief and even of comfort will be obtained by consulting a second opinion, as it were, upon its perplexing case, in the other the much-dreaded ordeal, the pain and shame of confession, are supposed to constitute powerful safeguards against the repetition of the offence.  Our comparison would be incomplete if we did not add that in the one case the confession is encouraged or permitted with a view to the removal of a recognized obstacle existing between the soul and Christ, while in the other it is required with a view to the imposing of penance and the pronouncing of " sacramental absolution."

Having thus, to save ourselves from being misunderstood or misinterpreted, pointed out the distinction between things that *do* differ in their most essential features, and scarcely resemble each other more closely than " Monmouth and Macedon," we pass on to consider the case of those who find their difficulty at this point. It cannot be too emphatically stated that repentance is impossible while we continue in our hearts to cling to known sin. Our Church Catechism teaches this very forcibly when it employs the phrase " repentance whereby we forsake sin : " there is no real repentance without this. Here, however, we must be careful to point out the distinction between forsaking sin and overcoming sin. To be willing to part company with our sins is one thing, to be able to conquer them is quite another. God's grace cannot enter our hearts till the first point is gained ; nothing but God's grace already in full possession can enable us to gain the second. The point to be decided by the awakened sinner is not whether he is able to save himself from his sin, but whether he is willing to let the Lord Jesus fulfil his own prophetic Name, by saving him from his sins ; and if he find a difficulty at this point, we would suggest to him the expediency of reflecting upon the real character of sin. Let such an one ask himself whether sin has really brought him happiness or misery in the past and the present, and from the lessons of experience let him judge of what the future rewards of iniquity are likely to be. Let him weigh whatever of gratification he may have derived from his most cherished vice or infirmity against all his other present and eternal interests, and remember that to cling to the former is certainly to make shipwreck of the latter. Let him consider that he is courting slavery, and turning his back upon true liberty; for sin only assumes the part of an obsequious slave in order that it may become a tyrant; like the aspirant for the Roman purple, whose mode of conduct Tacitus describes in a single sentence " *Omnia serviliter pro imperio ;* " and let him ponder well that inexorable law, " Whatsoever a man soweth, that shall he also reap."

But it is the cross of Christ that offers the most powerful argument to decide the wavering soul. There we see, as in a stupendous object-lesson, what the wages of sin must needs be, and the thought is pressed home upon us with irresistible force how baleful must be the bondage from which God was content to redeem us at such a price nor can we avoid the startling reflection,—if God

spared not His own Son when that Son represented human sin, how can He spare us if we
continue to cling to that from which He died to
save us? And even that is not all; the strength
of sin lies in the thought that it ministers to our
enjoyment, and that in denying it to us God is
jealous of our happiness. All such blasphemous
suspicions are silenced by this one supreme manifestation of Divine love. He who has exhibited
the measure of His love for man in His " unspeakable gift," cannot be indifferent to the happiness
of creatures whom He so highly favours. Such
love as His must surely aim, not at robbing us
of enjoyment, but at opening up to us the purest
and deepest delight that the creature is capable of;
so that the sinner need not fear, with Calvary before
his eyes, to turn his back upon the most cherished
sin. Having witnessed such a revelation of a Father's
love he cannot be wrong in counting all things loss
that come between him and his enjoyment of this.

Still more frequently it happens that the soul
is kept back from Christ *by its reluctance to forsake
the world.* The objects to which it clings may
not be in themselves morally wrong, yet it cannot
but feel that they would be weights and hindrances
in a Christian's course.

Perhaps it is the pleasures and the delirious excitement of worldly life that holds the captive spellbound, perhaps the love of money, or the dreams of political or commercial ambition; in any case it is suggested to the mind that there is a great deal to be given up for Christ, so much that life will lose half its charms if the decisive choice be made. To such we need to point out that they are scarcely in a position as yet to judge what sacrifices may really have to be made; they may themselves be surprised to find by-and-by that the things which they now prize so highly have become strangely depreciated in value by the acquisition of something better. When St. Paul turned his back on all things, he counted them but loss for the excellency of the knowledge of Christ Jesus his Lord. In after years he looked upon such sacrifices with no regretful eye—*we none of us object to lose loss*—and how often have we listened to similar expressions on the lips of young Christians. I thought, such an one will often be heard to say, that I should find it very hard to give up what I before loved so dearly, but somehow I find all my pleasure in these things at an end. It is not now that *I must not*, but that *I would not;* I have found something better, and "no man having drunk the old wine straightway desireth new."

It is well to count the cost, but by all means let us count both the cost and the profits on both sides, or our conclusion is sure to be vicious. Since, however, the soul at this point is scarcely in a position to decide what will and what will not have to be given up, nor to estimate the amount of pain that such sacrifices will entail, his wisdom will lie in simply confiding these matters to the care of a loving and sympathising God, taking it for certain that he cannot be really a loser, whatever he may be called upon to give up. Let the will be decided to "win Christ," cost what it may, and then the consideration of details can be left until we have felt what Chalmers so well calls "the expulsive power of a new affection."

Cases of this kind sometimes occur in which the tenderest feelings of our nature are involved. Not unfrequently, and especially in the case of young people, a cherished attachment seems to stand in the way of full decision for Christ, and here the Master's call seems to ask for something dearer than life itself. Surely such cases, above all others, claim our deepest sympathy, and need to be treated with a very gentle hand, and with much prudence and caution, lest in the one case we should induce the conviction that worldly alliances can be permitted without grievous detriment to the spiritual life, or on the other, unduly discourage the seeking soul by setting before him the necessity of making tremendous sacrifices which perhaps may never be called for.

In fact, it is only right and natural that he who is awakened under such circumstances should entertain the strongest desire and hope of winning over the object of his affection to Christ, nor would he be the more likely to effect this purpose by beginning with something like a threat of breaking off all previously existing relations. At no time in life has one person more influence over another than at this, and if this do not prevail when a kind but firm stand has been taken, the question is most likely to settle itself, without any such definite act of self-sacrifice as might at first have been apprehended. For the entire absence of inward sympathy tends to produce estrangement even between those who once were most passionately attached to each other, and it becomes obvious on both sides that nothing but pain and disappointment can accrue from a union so ill-matched and incomplete.

Let it however be laid down for certain that the claims of Jesus Christ upon the human heart are paramount, and he that loves father or mother, wife or sister, more than his Lord, is not worthy of Him; yet He who makes this claim assures us that we shall be no losers, even in this life; the Lord undertakes to compensate a hundredfold all who have made any such sacrifice for Him. Let those who waver at this point consider whether either they themselves, or those on whom their affections are fixed, are likely to be gainers in real happiness and true well-being, either here or hereafter, by a decision in which the creature is set before the Creator; and whether a union can possibly be blessed or even happy, the condition of which is the repudiation of the claims of Christ. In how many a dismal tragedy of domestic life do we discern the fruits of such a fatal choice, and perhaps the results are in the end most appalling where they are at present least apparent.

# CHAPTER IX.

## A LAST OBSTACLE TO DECISION, AND THE FIRST STEP OF THE DECIDED.

BEFORE we pass on from the consideration of those difficulties which beset the definite act of decision of will on the part of the awakened sinner, we must needs refer to one cause which, perhaps more than any other, keeps a large number of persons from the acceptance of the Gospel blessing. If appearances are to be trusted, more awakened souls are kept back from Christ by pride than by any other barrier that the ingenuity of the enemy has devised. This generally takes the form of a false, unmanly shame; the understanding is convinced, the feelings are greatly stirred, but the contempt and ridicule of the world has to be faced. The bewildered soul, distracted by opposing emotions, seems to become so morally paralysed as to be incapable of definite action. What will people say? how my friends will despise me! how shall I ever hold up my head again in society? how can I bring myself to be a butt for the ridicule of those who have hitherto respected and perhaps even admired me? These are the thoughts that seem to take possession of the mind with over-whelming force, and for the moment to neutralize all better aspirations and more worthy considerations.

We may point out in passing that the existence of this difficulty is in itself a singular and noteworthy phenomenon. No other religion, so far as we know, excites any similar feeling in those who desire to profess it, or provokes an attitude on the part of others that might account for any such feeling. On the contrary, the believers in pagan and other false systems are proud of their religion, and are much more disposed to parade it than to conceal it. It is also remarkable that this feeling is stronger amongst nominal Christians, just in so far as the type of Christianity presented to them is pure and spiritual. A carnal and super-stitious form of Christianity does not awaken a sense of shame, nor are men kept back from embracing it by any such emotion.

This fact demands an explanation, and in the consideration of that explanation which we believe to be the true one, the wavering heart may find an argument which should tell against its indecision. This feeling of shame is surely due to the fact that the " prince of this world " puts out of his court, as it were, and endeavours to cover with obloquy, all who surrender themselves to the world's rightful Ruler, and so reject his own usurped authority. To confess allegiance to David is to make ourselves unpopular at the court of Absalom; but those who are held at this point should reflect what it is that they will be doing if they yield to this feeling of shame. They will be dishonouring and disowning Him whose love has already aroused their once slumbering hearts, and placing themselves, like another Ahithophel or Shimei, at the disposal of the tyrant and the usurper. Let such reflect whether it is not something to be indeed ashamed of to take sides with the powers of evil in the great moral struggle which divides the world, and whether it is not worse than despicable to make decision for the world, with the full intention of turning in an hour of need to Him whom we have rejected and disowned.

It is worthy of notice that our Lord seems to have bound together with special care, so that no man can put them asunder, these two moral acts,

8

belief and confession. He claims it in the most definite language of all who listen to His teaching, that they should not be ashamed to confess Him before men. "Whosoever," He exclaims in His most solemn and emphatic manner, "shall be ashamed of Me and of My words in this adulterous and sinful generation, of him shall the Son of man be ashamed when He cometh in the glory of His Father, with His holy angels." Similar to this is the teaching of St. Paul, when, in that passage which we may perhaps regard as the *locus classicus* with respect to the subjective conditions of justification, he lays it down that "if thou shalt confess with thy mouth the Lord Jesus, and believe in thine heart that God raised Him from the dead, thou shalt be saved." It is well then that those who are kept back by the fear of man that bringeth a snare should remember that if they are ever to be Christians at all, sooner or later the open confession must be made, and therefore surely the sooner the better. It does not grow easier but harder to commit oneself to a decided course of action by delaying decision, whereas one bold and determined act may give the death blow to the power of shame within the human heart for ever.

This circumstance may be pleaded as an apology,

if not as a justification, for a method of dealing
with awakened souls sometimes adopted at missions, but more frequently at Methodist revivals,
which is usually perhaps too hastily and incon-
siderately condemned by those who do not discern
the purpose that it is designed to subserve. We
refer to the practice of setting apart a certain
place in the building in which the service is being
held for those who are really seeking, and calling
upon all who belong to that class to rise before
the eyes of the congregation, and proceed to the
place thus chosen. This is to many a very severe
ordeal, and it may naturally be questioned whether
the evangelist is right, or, at any rate, wise, in
subjecting those in whom new and better desires
are only just beginning to exist, to so severe a
test; but this much must be admitted, that such a
mode of procedure is really much less cruel than
at first sight it appears to be; for while it may
cost a great effort at the moment to take so public
a step, who shall say how much difficulty such
an act may save us afterwards? Men know what
to expect of those who are thus content to become
fools for Christ, and hence we are spared in a
great measure the pain of having to take up a
new line of conduct towards old friends: the fact

is, that usually they, hearing of this openly avowed change in us, are the first to adopt new courses towards us. We have made fools of ourselves, and we must be treated accordingly.

At any rate, we would strongly advise those who are aware that their chief hindrance is shame, to adopt a very decisive line of conduct. One bold act performed without reference to consequences will often break this chain altogether, while, on the other hand, the longer we trifle with it the more confirmed the bondage must become. We need to be reminded that pride is a prominent form of *sin*, and that since true repentance, as we have seen, is characterized by the forsaking of sin, we cannot really repent while we cling to this. It is often the case that the soul that has been deterred by this finds itself unable to obtain the peace and comfort it desires, however earnestly it may seek it in privacy and solitude. This besetting sin has to be renounced, and until this is done by some overt act, the heart not unfrequently fails to find any rest.

Two or three thoughts suggest themselves as likely to be useful to those with whom pride and shame are the obstacles that keep them from Christ. It will be well for such to reflect on the unmanliness and miserable littleness of such moral cowardice. We despise the soldier who flinches on the battle-field, but surely not less, but more despicable is the fault of him who falters on the moral battle-field, not because his judgment is not convinced, but simply because he fears the sneer of the world. As we find, remarkably enough, that it is frequently those who are rather disposed to plume themselves on their manhood who fall into this snare, some good results might doubtless ensue if men would reflect on its true moral character. Next, such persons need to be reminded that shame cannot be escaped where it is for a time evaded. The sure word of prophecy informs us that "many of them that sleep in the dust of the earth shall arise, some to everlasting life, and some to shame and everlasting contempt." We have thus to make our choice between exposing ourselves to a little short-lived ridicule from a few frivolous and probably empty-headed acquaintances, for whose opinions on moral and religious subjects we ourselves possibly entertain no kind of respect, and the everlasting contempt which shall overwhelm the awakened consciousness in that last dread moment when Divine Wisdom must needs "mock at our calamity," and we shall as much despise ourselves, as we shall be found an " abhorring to all flesh."

Most of all, surely, it may serve to raise us above such moral poltroonery when we reflect that He who calls upon us not to be ashamed of Him is the same Who for our sakes " endured the cross and despised the shame." We shall never be exposed to such scorn and contempt as was hurled at our blessed Master; we shall never have the further trial of possessing, as He unquestionably did, all through His most grievous humiliation the power to exchange His shame for glory, and the contumely heaped upon Him by sinners for the adoring homage of angels; yet for our sakes He despised the shame. Surely He has a right to claim it of us that we who owe so much to His moral courage should be ready to share His reproach; and it is not too much to expect that where a mere sense of duty and even of manhood may fail, the enthusiasm inspired by personal gratitude may yet prevail to lead us to become ashamed of our own shame, and to turn from this dumb idol of self-esteem to Him the living God.

When the difficulties which beset the action of the will at this point have been surmounted, much has been gained; to us it always seems that the victory is more than half won. We remember, however, that in our favourite type, the prodigal son, the utterance of decision is described as being immediately followed by the act of decision; the determination, " I will arise," by the statement, "and he arose." A mere resolution that we will seek after God will prove of little value unless it be promptly followed by the act of seeking; indeed, it may do more harm than good.

It is at this point, when the will is decided, and that decision seeks some definite expression, that the religious instincts of the soul, and we feel persuaded we may add, the gracious influences of the Holy Spirit, will usually lead us to betake ourselves to earnest, agonizing prayer. The soul has reached its Penuel, and finds itself alone with God, and with all the energy that it can command it endeavours to wrestle for the longed-for blessing. Like the patriarch of old the seeking soul "weeps and makes supplication," and dares to exclaim in its agony of desire, " I will not let Thee go except Thou bless me."

We have heard it very strenuously urged by some, in whose case we are constrained to think that dogmatism has overridden sound judgment, that it is an error to advise seeking souls to pray.

It is argued that prayer is the breath of the living soul. and cannot be in its proper place in the mouth of those who are spiritually dead; that the New Testament directions call upon the awakened soul to repent and believe, but not to pray—nay, further, that prayer under such circumstances is positively misleading, as it disposes the soul to fix its attention rather on something that is to be done, than upon the great work of redemption already accomplished. All this sounds very consistent, and is no doubt very plausible, but such teaching is based upon a partial and one-sided view of truth, which, as usual, is the parent of error. It is quite true that the soul that is out of Christ is *spiritually* dead; that is to say, is cut off from all vital union with God, the only Source of true spiritual vitality; it is equally true that *morally* it is alive, and hence capable of moral action, and to this capacity God makes His appeal.

What response to that appeal can be more rational than that the soul awakened to its sense of need should pour forth its desires in fervent supplication? Such earnest entreaty is a very different thing from that prayer of the wicked which Holy Scripture tells us is an abomination to the Lord; the prayer there referred to is obviously the prayer of one who is cleaving to his sins while he performs the outward exercises of devotion. The cry for help of the awakened sinner arises from his wish to be saved from his sins. It is natural to us, in our dealings with each other, to ask for that of which we feel our need: the starving man asks for bread, the drowning man asks for assistance, and the child that has offended its parent asks for pardon. Surely God desires us to act in accordance with the instincts of our nature in seeking for spiritual blessings.

But we are not left merely to the conclusions of common sense in this matter; the plain teaching of Holy Scripture, in both the Old and New Testaments, seems to justi y these conclusions. In the Old Testament the prophet Hosea puts into the mouth of the repentant sinner the very words that God would have him use in turning to the Lord: " Take with you words, and turn unto the Lord, and say unto Him, Take away all iniquity, receive us graciously;" and the fifty-first psalm is as eloquent and appropriate an utterance for the seeking soul as is the hundred and third psalm for him who has found. If it be argued that the case is different under the new Dispensation, we reply that our blessed Lord surely affords us a sufficient warrant for this mode of procedure in His parable of the publican and the Pharisee; nay, we may say He puts into the sinner's lips, in this remarkable passage, the very prayer above all others that is appropriate to his condition, "God be merciful to me *the* sinner." We may observe further, that in most of those instances in which Christ exercised His healing power He was approached with supplications; and these incidents are surely set forth as examples or types of the grander miracles of grace which belong to this Dispensation. If He did not reprove their petitions, neither will He, we may argue with some confidence, reprove our prayers.

But a still more direct answer is given to such teaching by the case of Saul of Tarsus, whose conversion we may regard in many respects as a typical one. Of him it is stated by our Lord Himself, as the reason why Ananias should at once proceed to him, "Behold, he prayeth;" and in our blessed Lord's benignant exultation over this fact we find reason for concluding that Saul was doing the thing most appropriate to his condition at the moment. It will be evident, on a careful examination of the recorded facts of the case, that Saul of Tarsus was earnestly seeking, and not rejoicing over having found salvation during those three dark days spent in the street called Strait, and hence he occupied himself as a seeker naturally would in earnest prayer, and the Lord speaks of this course with evident satisfaction and approval.

We have so little told us of the method pursued by the Apostles in dealing with individual souls, that we have to be guided rather by inferences of this kind than by direct statements, but it is worthy of notice that in one instance, at any rate, prayer is distinctly recommended by an Apostle to a man whom he has himself just pronounced to have neither part nor lot in real spiritual experience, and whose heart was not right with God. "Repent of this thy wickedness, and pray God if perhaps the thought of thine heart may be forgiven thee." Surely, if prayer was appropriate in the case of so doubtful a penitent as Simon Magus, it cannot be out of place in the case of any sincere and honest inquirer.

But, it may be asked, what is the use of prayer under such circumstances? and what beneficial purpose may it justly be expected to subserve? It cannot be too clearly understood that prayers and entreaties are not required to melt the heart of an unsympathetic God, even as a hard-hearted man may sometimes be moved by the agonizing importunity of a suppliant. God's heart is too full of love and mercy to need any melting, and His provision to meet our needs is perfect, even before our needs are expressed. Prayer is useful chiefly because it provides, as it were, an expression for penitence. It helps the seeking soul to realize that it is against a Person that he has sinned, not merely against a law or an abstract principle, and brings him into direct contact with that Person. It enables him to form a more definite apprehension of what his want really is, and thus prepares him for claiming the blessing he needs. When blind Bartimæus approached our Lord, he was asked, "What wilt thou that I should do unto thee?" not because his wishes were at all likely to be indefinite upon this subject, much less because our Lord Himself did not apprehend his need. Surely for our sakes was this written, that we might learn the importance to ourselves of thus definitely apprehending and expressing the desire which we would fain His grace should satisfy.

And this leads us to point out that the prayer of the true penitent will be very simple, very direct. He will be little disposed to employ verbose phrases and vague and roundabout forms of speech. He feels himself a perishing sinner, and he needs salvation, and to this point he will confine his petitions, with as much directness and simplicity of aim as would be exhibited by the man who cries for help when in danger of drowning. The cry for mercy, pardon, and salvation, blended with the confession of our sin, and of our incapacity to merit what we seek, will be the first most natural utterance of the awakened soul; and how often have we observed that the moment that the suppliant cry is raised, the heart that previously seemed almost incapable of feeling loses all its hardness, and often with tears of deep contrition, and sometimes with a fervency of desire not less precious than tears, the soul pours forth its pleadings into the pitying ear of its God.

Ere we close this chapter, in order to avoid misapprehensions, let us say that we have no intention of affirming that it is always necessary that the soul should pray before it can obtain peace, still less that it should spend days and even weeks in protracted supplication, as sometimes doubtless happens. We merely affirm that prayer of the kind we have described is generally found to be useful at this particular stage of spiritual experience, and suggests it as likely to be a help to those who, having made up their minds to seek salvation, scarcely know how to proceed. It is not indeed by prayer that salvation is to be obtained, nor is it for the most part in the act of prayer that the soul finds the comfort it seeks; prayer is not the condition of salvation, though it may lead on to compliance with that condition. Yet well is it with the awakened soul when a rejoicing Saviour, already anticipating the completion of the work that His Spirit has begun, can look down upon him and exclaim, " Behold, he prayeth."

# CHAPTER X.

## QUESTIONS AND DIFFICULTIES CONNECTED WITH REPENTANCE.

WE have so far followed the soul through the preliminary experiences of repentance up to the point of decision, and have spoken of the first step which the soul will most naturally be disposed to take as soon as that decision is made. Much is gained when the awakened sinner is brought to cast himself prostrate before the mercy-seat, and to humble himself before God while he confesses his sins and seeks for pardon. Difficulties, however, may still arise, and perplexities may still bewilder the soul even when this point has been reached, and indeed in some cases it is after this that the most painful experiences have to be encountered. The ruthless enemy makes a last stand, for well he knows that his dominion is at an end as soon as the soul finds the pardon and the peace that it is seeking, and endeavours by all the means at his command so to weary out and discourage the eager and longing soul, that it may be disposed to give up the search in despair.

In considering these questions and difficulties which may suggest themselves to the repentant soul, we will pursue the method adopted in a former chapter, and take for our headings questions that are frequently asked, and difficulties that are raised, by those who are passing through these experiences. Here are some of them :—

*" I cannot remember all my sins—how then can I confess them ? and if I don't confess them, how can they be forgiven ? "*

To this it might be enough to answer that God does not demand impossibilities, nor have we any reason to expect that we shall be supernaturally endowed with memory in order to enable us to obtain Divine mercy. But we prefer to point out that such a difficulty springs from an imperfect apprehension of the true nature of repentance—a misapprehension which the mediæval practice of auricular confession has done much to foster. Repentance consists of a change in the attitude of the soul towards God, and it is by no means dependent upon the recollection of particular acts of definite sin, though it is most frequently accompanied by this. The repentant sinner finds his whole life to have been one long sin, because it has been lived without God in the world. His very religion he finds has been one form of godlessness, because it has tended to satisfy his religious instincts with something less than the personal knowledge of God. In his most amiable and praiseworthy actions he discovers sin, just because they were sops to his conscience, or assertions of his moral independence of God. Where all is sin, some sins may wear a deeper shade than others, but it will be generally found that the true penitent bewails those sins most which have been more directly committed against God, and even contemplates those which have been definitely committed against man chiefly as offences against the Divine law and will. No man ever sinned more definitely and grievously against his neighbour than did David, and yet in his confession he seems to lose sight of his sin against man in the thought of his greater sin against God · " Against Thee only have I sinned and done this evil in Thy sight."

The Holy Spirit convinces of sin, because we believe not on Christ: not only of the sin of not trusting Christ, but of the fact that all other sins are due to this, because they would never have been committed had not this been committed, and that all other sins continue to stand against us because this sin stands against us. The effect of this is to produce a general, but not less overwhelming, sense of sin. The truth indeed is, not that we cannot remember our sins, but rather that we can hardly remember anything that has not been more or less infected by sin. So much is this the case, that in some of the most deep and genuine cases of repentance that have ever come under our notice, no single sin has so stood forth from amongst the rest as to attract special attention to itself; and we are bound to add that amongst the least satisfactory cases that we have ever known have been some in which the thought of one sin in particular has so engrossed the attention, that little sensibility has been left for the life-long sin from which all specific offences spring. What God desires is not, so to speak, a special apology for each particular sin, but the breaking down of our pride and the submission of our souls to Him in true humiliation and self-abasement; and when this takes place, we need not distress ourselves because our memory is frail and the details of our past lives have melted from our recollections.

*" But ought I not to make reparation before*
*I can hope to find forgiveness ? "*

This is a very reasonable and proper feeling,
and there are undoubtedly circumstances in which
reparation should be made, and in which it may
be regarded as one of the most certain fruits of
true repentance ; but it may be put in the wrong
place, and so become a hindrance instead of a help
to the seeking soul. First, we need hardly point
out that it is only to our fellow-man that it is
possible for us to make reparation ; to God our
debt is so great, that all thought of paying it is out
of the question. Indeed, it is only when we feel
that we have nothing to pay, that we are in a position to receive His frank forgiveness.

This is obvious enough to all who are familiar
with New Testament teaching ; but we need carefully to guard against falling into the mistake of
regarding practically, though not theoretically, acts
of reparation made to our fellow-man as a kind of
indirect reparation to God. We are no doubt apt
to allow ourselves to feel as if the shame and pain
that we submit to in making reparation to man
must be a kind of a *set-off* against our sin in the
eyes of God. And hence it may sometimes happen
that the awakened soul is eager to find some one

to whom it may make reparation, whether it be really called for or not, just because it fancies that such an act will be sure to bring it some inward relief and ease of conscience. We need to be reminded that it is possible to be self-righteous in the confession of unrighteousness, as well as in the assertion of our moral superiority.

It is only in certain instances that specific reparation is possible, and even in these it is not always possible at the moment. In all cases where we feel that our sins have injured society, we owe society the reparation of doing as much good as we can; but this must follow after a true conversion, and it would be preposterous to direct an awakened soul to wait till he had made amends to society before coming to Christ. But this *reductio ad absurdum* demonstrates to us what the true place of reparation is. It is not a meritorious act of self-mortification, designed to obtain the forgiveness of sin, or even as a step towards it, but a natural and necessary fruit of forgiveness, in cases where it is possible and to the degree in which it is possible.

If indeed the thought of the necessity of having to make just and reasonable reparation comes between the soul and God, it will doubtless be necessary to submit the soul in this respect to God before any peace can be obtained; but if this be honestly done, and we find ourselves *ready and willing*, by God's help, to do all that God calls upon us to do, we need not wait for the act of reparation to be made before we come to Christ, but rather come to Christ, that amongst other things we may obtain moral courage to make the act of reparation. Zacchæus first joyfully received Christ into his house, and probably into his heart, and then proceeded to make reparation. The disciples at Ephesus first believed in Christ, and then burned their books; which was probably as nearly an act of reparation as any that, under the circumstances, they could perform. It is not always possible to make full reparation; it is not every one that has the means to do what Zacchæus did; for such it is surely enough if they are ready to do what they can; they need not defer seeking and finding salvation until they have sufficiently increased their worldly store. This, like all other arguments for delay, is from beneath, not from above.

" *Others may be forgiven, but my sin is too great; I cannot believe that there is pardon for me.*"

This bitter and overwhelming despair is a dif

ferent thing from the somewhat reckless and super-ficial hopelessness which I described in a former chapter (see p. 83). It is experienced either by those who, being of a constitutionally melancholy temperament, are liable to intense depression when they come under the influence of conviction of sin, or by those whose consciences are weighted by some specially grievous crimes, or whose sins have been committed with deliberate determination, and against singular privileges. Great is the anguish that usually accompanies such experiences; and those cases are perhaps still more pitiable where instead of acute anguish there is calm fixed despair, as though the heart were turned to stone, and were capable of feeling no longer.

And yet one might suppose that there is enough in the New Testament to meet such doubts and set them at rest for ever. Surely they who are appalled at the magnitude of their sins might remember that they have still to do with "the Friend of publicans and sinners" and the Saviour of the lost. They might comfort themselves with the thought that on no occasion do we find our blessed Lord turning His back upon a sinner because of his sins, but that on the contrary we find Him holding out the hand of mercy to some of the very vilest of mankind. Are we not dishonouring the great Saviour, and limiting His omnipotent mercy, when we tell the Good Physician that our disease is too deadly for Him to cure? Does His atoning work avail only for the less serious offences of man? Can He save only those who come nearest to saving themselves, while He must needs leave the rest to perish? Surely the greatest criminals that have ever disgraced humanity are included in that vast "whosoever" that opens the gates of mercy to all mankind.

But while this is a sufficient answer for those who belong to the second class of persons that we have just described, those, namely, who have been guilty of some grievous crime, it does not equally meet the case of the others; indeed, the very text which of all others assures us of the possible pardon of the grossest sinner is not unfrequently supposed to shut out from the hope of salvation those whose sins are of a different order. "All manner of sin and blasphemy," says our blessed Lord, "shall be forgiven unto men, but the blasphemy against the Holy Ghost shall not be forgiven unto men." While this passage is absolutely conclusive as to the forgiveness of all other sins, whatever their character; while it holds out the most definite hope to the murderer, the adulterer, the profligate; the fact that it excepts one particular class of offences leads some persons of a morbid and despondent temperament to give place to the dread misgiving—

"*I fear that I have committed the unpardonable sin.*"

They come to this conclusion either because they have been tormented with blasphemous thoughts which have insisted on forcing their way into their minds, or because they feel, as they look back upon their past lives, that they have repeatedly resisted the gracious influences and motions of the Holy Spirit; and this they persuade themselves must be the sin against the Holy Ghost.

There are few passages probably in the New Testament more full of mystery, and more difficult of explanation, than this particular verse and its parallel passages; yet this much is obvious, that we have no right to make the passage say what it does not say. In all the Evangelists that give this remark of our Lord, it is not *a sin* but *a blasphemy* against the Holy Ghost that is spoken of. This should be a sufficient reply to a very considerable number of persons who are haunted with this fear, but who know perfectly well that their consciences accuse them of no such word or thought as could be described as blasphemy against the Divine Spirit, although they have often resisted and grieved Him.

But while this answer should settle the question in the case of those whose misgivings are to be attributed to the second of the two causes we have just mentioned, it does not meet the case of those who, whilst they have less real cause for apprehension, are most disposed to be dejected,—those, we mean, who are the victims of their own morbid experiences. Such will do well to reflect that there can be nothing arbitrary or inconsistent with what we may call the first principles of moral proportion in God's dealings with man. It is absurd to suppose that the most weighty and inexorable penalty shall be inflicted by a just God on account of any save the most grievous of offences ; and to give sin such a quality, it is clear that it must be committed with the deliberate purpose and full moral intent of the sinner. The last sin to deserve such a punishment (if it be a sin at all) would be an unwelcomed and intrusive thought, that we shrink from with aversion, even at the moment that it thrusts itself into our minds. Whatever the sin against the Holy Ghost may be, it must be the sin of a most determinedly dishonest and wilfully untruthful heart; it cannot be the error of a perplexed intellect, or the morbid nightmare of an ungoverned imagination.

It is no doubt true that there comes a time in the impenitent sinner's life when the Divine Spirit ceases to strive with him, and he is left alone; but callous indifference and reckless apathy are far more likely to be the indications that this condition has been reached, than agonizing fears, cruel remorse, and harrowing misgivings. Let those who are conscious that their guilt is great, and that they have sinned against God's Holy Spirit, find comfort in the thought that the presence of such a conviction is an unmistakable proof that they have not yet been abandoned by the Convictor, and let them make haste, while these gracious influences last, to yield to His call, and cast themselves on the mercy of God in Christ.

There is another still more common difficulty connected with repentance, which frequently distresses and impedes those who are already awakened, and it may be thus expressed,—

*" I cannot feel any adequate sorrow for sin. I wish to repent, but my heart is hard and insensible."*

This difficulty is usually based upon the mistaken notion that repentance consists in feeling sorrow for sin ; if this were true, a very serious barrier would indeed exist between the soul and God, for who can so command his own emotions as to be able to feel sorrow whenever he wishes to do so? If this were the case, it would indeed be strange that the call to repent should be uttered as a command no less than ten times in New Testament Scriptures. We might well reply that we were asked to compass an impossibility, if the word repent meant " feel sorrow." But the truth is, that though a greater or less amount of sorrow or regret always does accompany repentance, the repentance and the sorrow are quite distinct from each other. Sometimes the sorrow is the cause of the repentance, according to St. Paul's statement, " Godly sorrow worketh repentance," and sometimes it flows from repentance as a result, as in the case of David, where all the plaintive and sorrowful utterances of the fifty-first Psalm followed on his repentance and forgiveness.

On the other hand, it is possible that there may be great sorrow for sin, particularly for some special sin, without any real repentance, and there may be real repentance when the soul complains against itself, because it does not feel the sorrow that it desires ; but the two things are quite distinct from each other, and none need think that their repentance cannot be accepted by God because they don't feel as much sorrow as they would wish.

But let us endeavour to inquire as closely as we can into the nature of this objection, and the attitude of soul that it betrays. Is there not in this intense desire to feel an adequate sorrow for sin a subtle and well-concealed form of that disposition to do something to merit salvation, which is ever ready in one way or another to assert itself? If we cannot win Divine favour with our works, at any rate we may claim some consideration on account of the depth of our contrition and the intensity of our distress. Now whenever such a feeling as this is present to our mind, it is not to be wondered at that God in His dealings with us should deny us those very emotions which we most wish to feel. He sees our disposition to regard them as, in some degree, the purchase money of pardon, and since He has to train us to true views of our dependence on Him in the very act of showing mercy upon us, it is not surprising if He finds Himself constrained to withhold the inward experiences which perhaps might have been ours but for our disposition to trust in them.

There is nothing expiatory in our sorrow for sin. We have not to descend into the depths, for that would be to bring Christ up again from the dead. Enduring our sorrow, as well as carrying our sin, the great Representative of mankind fathomed that depth for us. He apprehended the true character of sin, as we cannot with our less delicate sensibilities; and yet for our sakes was content to be identified with that which His soul abhorred. Though He had never grieved His Father, yet He was permitted to feel Himself under the cloud of Divine displeasure, as though He had. God's rebuke broke His human heart, and in the anguish which He thus endured we do indeed see adequate sorrow for sin.

If sin is to be expiated by sorrow, it is His sorrow, not ours, that must offer the expiation. But the expiation has been made. Christ is no longer under the cloud of darkness and death; and when we tarry in our approach to the mercy-seat for adequate sorrow for sin, we are forgetting

this, and, as the Apostle teaches, practically endeavouring to bring up Christ again from the
dead; for we are acting as though we would
imply that His expiatory sorrows are not sufficient,
but require to be supplemented by our adequate
sorrow for sin, before He and we in Him can be
accepted before God.

But it may be asked, Is it then a matter of
indifference whether we feel sorrow for sin or not?
We reply, By no means.   Repentance is not the
mere perfunctory utterance of what may be termed
spiritual apologies, it is impossible for us honestly
to turn our backs upon our past life, and to confess our sin against our greatest Benefactor, without
feeling some sense of painful regret or contrition;
but we shall not deepen or increase such emotions
by contemplating them; on the contrary, the less
we think about our own feeling of sorrow, the
more likely it is to be deep and genuine; and it
is for the most part just because the persons
whose case we are considering are so intensely
introspective, that they are so little personally
conscious of the sorrow which no doubt to a
greater or less degree they actually do feel, though
they will not admit it.   If, instead of weighing
their own feelings and analysing their own motives

such persons would only "look unto Him whom they have pierced," they would soon mourn "for Him as one mourneth for an only son" (Zech. xii. 10); for it is this that produces real sorrow for sin, it is this that breaks the heart—the thought of what our sins have cost Him who voluntarily consented to bear them for us, the thought of His generous love contrasted with our black ingratitude. Above all, let such seeking souls remember that their tears and anguish are not required to melt the obdurate heart of an unsympathetic God; that heart is love, and needs no melting, but is already yearning with an intensity of desire over all His rebellious and alienated children.

Let us point out, ere we close this chapter, that all these arguments for delay bear on their very surface the stamp of the quarter from which they proceed. It is not the habit of our Father God to keep returning prodigals waiting outside the gate. In the parable to which we have so often referred, " when the son was yet a great way off, the father saw him, and ran, and fell on his neck, and kissed him." " Thou, Lord, art good," exclaims the Psalmist, " and *ready to forgive,*" so ready that forgiveness must needs reach us as soon as we are ready to be forgiven. Surely if this last point could only be gained with all, the whole human family might at once be rejoicing in His pardoning grace; for God keeps none waiting.

# CHAPTER XI.

## QUESTIONS AND DIFFICULTIES CONNECTED WITH FAITH.

FAITH in God through Jesus Christ has been appointed by Divine wisdom as the condition on man's side of the justification of the human soul. Holy Scripture knows much of free, but nothing of *unconditional* salvation, though that phrase is sometimes incautiously employed by those who are eager to exalt God's part in this matter, perhaps somewhat at the expense of man's. The word condition, however, may be misleading, because the conditions on which benefits are bestowed by man on men are usually such as imply, more or less, the idea of a return or recompense, and it is most important clearly to apprehend that faith is not a price that we pay, nor a meritorious duty that we perform; rather it is the expression of the soul's inability to pay a price, or fulfil its duty, and therefore of its decision to cast itself unreservedly

10

upon Divine grace. Faith is that attitude of the soul towards God in which it is possible for it to become the recipient of Divine blessing; it is the stretching out of the hand to receive a gift, not the earning of that gift by the dexterous exercise of certain spiritual faculties.

We may perhaps, without irreverence, form a rational assumption as to the reasons that determined Divine wisdom to introduce this particular condition, and no other, into the terms of justification. God might have appointed prayer, fasting, almsgiving, or a variety of other conditions; but it is evident that any of these would, first, have conveyed a false impression to the mind of the penitent, leading him to attribute his own salvation, more or less, to himself; and, second, would not have necessarily insured that inward apprehension of the redeeming work of Christ, from which the soul is to derive its constraining motive and its new life-power tor its subsequent spiritual experiences. Above all, these conditions would not have led us necessarily right back, as it were, into the outstretched arms of the God from whom we have wandered; as Christ died "to bring us to God," so faith in God through Christ is the step that takes us home. Faith then, it would seem, has been ordained as the condition of justification on man's side, first, because it can in no sense be regarded as a meritorious work ; next, because in the act of exercising it our attention is drawn to all the great lessons which the atonement is designed to convey; and next, because the very act of faith draws us out of ourselves, away from our self-consciousness, and brings our hearts to rest in God. We may add, that faith would seem to be demanded because it specially honours Christ, leading the soul to assume to the Saviour a moral attitude similar to that which has been adopted towards Him by God Himself, as a line of one of our hymns well puts it—

"God rests in Thee—in Thee I rest."

We may also say that a merciful God has appointed this as being really the simplest and easiest of all conditions, so that no poor weary sinner should be constrained to turn away from the gate of mercy because he could not comply with the terms on which the benefit is offered.

With this last thought fresh in our minds it may seem strange to have to confess that here also the ground is beset with difficulties, yet must it be frankly admitted that this is the case; here, as

elsewhere, the perverse ingenuity of man has interfered with the beneficent operations of the counsels
of God's love on his behalf, and he has contrived
to construct barriers between himself and God, out
of that very provision which was designed to sweep
all barriers away. It is no uncommon thing to
hear an awakened soul speak as though, of all
conceivable contrivances for keeping man out of
the enjoyment of God's favour, that which God
has actually appointed were the most skilfully
designed for this end, as though indeed God were
disposed to tantalize us by bringing salvation all
but within our reach, and then withdrawing it from
us by imposing an impossible condition, which pre-
cludes us from accepting what we so much need
and desire.

In our endeavour to clear away the difficulties
of this order, which still stand between the repentant
soul and Christ, we will first of all spend a few
moments in considering what the nature of that
faith is which God demands, and upon which
justification depends, and here we will suppose
ourselves met with the difficulty,

*" God requires me to believe with my heart.
I am afraid that I have not the right kind of faith."*

They who raise this difficulty are generally impressed with the idea that true faith is something very mysterious and perplexing, and that when the Bible uses the word it means something by it entirely distinct from what we are accustomed to indicate by the term when we apply it to other objects. We have no difficulty in understanding what it is to believe with our hearts in physician, or statesman, or man of business; but we persuade ourselves that a moral experience, quite distinct from this, not merely as to its object, but as to its intrinsic character, is required before we can be said to have faith in Christ.

But why should we suppose that God, in making a revelation of His mercy to us, lays Himself out to bewilder us, by using words in a mysterious and non-natural sense, and that, too, without guiding, even by a definition? how can we be blamed for taking the words to mean just what they usually mean, instead of something altogether inexplicable and peculiar, especially when God's Word sounds no note of warning upon the subject? We may feel perfectly sure that faith as a certain moral attitude of the soul is essentially the same, to whatever object it may be directed, and that the only difference between faith in God and faith in man lies in this, that the former may be much more sure and steadfast, just because the Object is more trustworthy. All that is required with respect to our faith is that it should be *complete* and full, and be exercised by our whole being, and not merely by one element of it.

To make this clear, but not to give the idea that faith is something very elaborate, let us endeavour to analyse true faith into its constituent elements, which we shall find to correspond to the intellectual, moral, and emotional elements in our own complex nature. In the act of believing, there will be, first, the intellectual apprehension of the object, be it what it may, towards which our faith is directed. In justification, that Object is the Lord Jesus Christ. On Him the mind rests; and we see in Him a full provision to meet our helpless case. We contemplate His double relations, with God on the one hand, with us sinners on the other; we consider His character, we acknowledge His work, we recognize His office, and discern in Him the Saviour of the world. But so far we may go, and yet there shall be only "head faith," that is, an intellectual apprehension of truth, and we may find ourselves as far from Christ, personally, as ever.

The second element in a true act of faith will

be the decision of the will to repose moral confidence in that which the mind has apprehended; and in justification, the next and all-important step is taken when the will decides to repose its confidence in the Person and work of Christ, as meeting all its needs, and assuring it of present salvation, and that without reference to any inward and sensible experiences of an unusual or supernatural order. We do not see, we do not feel, perhaps, but God is true, and we will trust in Him, come what may. And thus to every doubtful thought, to every misgiving and fear, we reply with calm assurance that we are persuaded that Jesus Christ is trustworthy, and we have left ourselves in His hands : he who seeks to trouble us must first apply to Him into whose hands we have committed our souls.

We are thus led on to the third element in a true act of faith, a certain inward sense of calm confidence, springing from the assurance that what we have trusted to the trustworthy is secure; and in justification this takes the form of an inward consciousness of rest, and a feeling of relief in the assurance that we have now nothing to fear; we have trusted ourselves into the Everlasting Arms, and he that believeth on Him shall not be ashamed.

A simple illustration may serve to make all this plain, and also to show that there is nothing very elaborate or mysterious in what we have been saying. A drowning man, struggling for his life, is approached by a strong swimmer who asks him to cease from struggling, and he will save him. The drowning man from the first has an intellectual conviction of the willingness and ability of the swimmer to save him; but it seems to him like instant death to give up struggling, and leave himself in another's hands. It is only by a definite act of the will that he can bring himself to trust his deliverer, and to prove his trust by an utter cessation of all his futile efforts to save himself; but the moment he actually does commit himself, provided he can only be perfectly sure of the ability and will of that other to save him, there must ensue a sense of relief and confidence of security which would not be interfered with by the thought that he was still in twenty fathoms of water, and fifty yards from the nearest land. Such an one as he, resting on his deliverer, without a misgiving as to the issue, is a good example of what is meant by heart faith. Let those who complain that their faith is only head faith ask hemselves why they should not take definite moral action upon that which with their heads they apprehend, and as soon as they do ,they will find themselves in assured possession of all that belongs to the true believer. But here another may perhaps inquire,

"*Is not true faith the gift of God? and must I not wait until it is bestowed?*"

Let us first endeavour to understand what the question means. The faculty of believing upon sufficient evidence, and of trusting where trust is warranted by circumstances, is certainly one of the original gifts of God to man, just as the faculties of knowing, imagining, loving, remembering, are gifts from Him; but inasmuch as these are gifts which He bestows in greater or less degree on all, nothing can be more absurd than to wait for them to be given over again, instead of employing them when occasion demands it. But the objection suggests that possibly, although the faculty of faith so far belongs to me by nature that I should be prepared, if expedient, voluntarily to put my life into the hands of the surgeon as I took my place on the operator's table, I need some further endowment before I can trust myself to Christ. Is this really so? And if so, where are the proofs of so astonishing a position in that Book which is our only guide to a true conclusion in such matters? If true faith be a directly supernatural gift, without which it is impossible to accept salvation, it does seem passing strange that faith should always have been claimed and demanded by the first Gospel teachers—that men should invariably have been told to believe, and never to pray or *to wait* for faith.

If faith is a supernatural gift, I cannot understand how St. Paul could say to the jailer at Philippi, "Believe on the Lord Jesus Christ, and thou shalt be saved." It is incredible that in no single instance seeking souls should have been told to ask God to give them saving faith. This is just one of those cases in which a negative argument is necessarily conclusive; for had the practice of giving any such strange and perplexing direction prevailed in those days, we needs must have found some trace of it. In most cases it will be found that this misconception is due to a mistaken exegesis of an important passage in one of St. Paul's epistles (Eph. ii. 8), where we read "By grace ye are saved through faith, and that not of yourselves; it is the gift of God." It is not surprising that the words as they stand in the English should have conveyed the idea that St. Paul here designed to affirm that saving faith is in a special sense the gift of God ; but the Greek Testament student will see at once that there is no kind of grammatical connection between the word " faith " and the word " that," the one being of the feminine gender, and the other of the neuter. Nor is there the slightest contextual ground for straining grammar to support such an interpretation; on the contrary, such a rendering of the passage would distort the whole argument, and produce a most irrelevant clause into the line of the Apostle's thoughts.

Introduce the word *salvation* after " that," and the whole passage is self-consistent, and I may add truly, Pauline : " By grace ye are saved through faith, and that salvation not of yourselves ; it is the gift of God, not of works, lest any man should boast ; " but substitute the word faith for the word salvation, and the argument at once halts and becomes inconsecutive : " By grace ye are saved through faith, and that faith not of yourselves ; it is the gift of God, not of works, lest any man should boast." We can scarcely fail to conclude that the parallel phrases, " not of yourselves," and " not of works," refer to the same object ; if that be faith, we need scarcely to be told that it is not of works ; indeed. such a sentence would be nonsense; if it be salvation, we have a strong and characteristic statement of Pauline doctrine. We conclude then with the fullest conviction that St. Paul designed to teach here that salvation (not faith) is God's free gift.

Of course there is a certain sense in which faith, like every right action or even holy thought, is a gift from God: but for the influences of His Holy Spirit, faith is the last thing we should be disposed to exercise; but this does not in the least interfere with our position that faith is not to be regarded as an extraordinary and supernatural faculty, for the gift of which we have to wait; but rather as a very simple attitude of the soul, which, in obedience to the influences of the Holy Spirit, we are bound to adopt. Before passing on, we may just observe that there is such a thing as a special gift of faith, which is mentioned in the catalogue of Christian gifts, side by side with the gifts of healing and prophecy and tongues, but our salvation no more depends on our possessing this, than upon our possessing the power to work miracles. If these conclusions be accepted, we can still imagine the troubled soul proceeding to ask—

*" But how am I to believe ?    I wish to, and yet seem unable."*

No better answer can be given than one that comes from an Apostle's pen: "So then faith cometh by hearing, and hearing by the word of God" (Rom. x. 17). If it comes by hearing, it does not come by waiting for it, or hoping for it, or praying for it. It comes by hearing; but what the hearing is to be, we may gather from the passage. St. Paul has just been quoting the opening words of the fifty-third chapter of Isaiah: "Who hath believed our report?" And then he goes on to say, "Faith comes from report." What the report is that is to elicit our faith as by a mystic spell, those who love this chapter, the best in the Bible, know full well; but perhaps we need to have enforced still more upon our mind that faith has its proper origin, not in any mere subjective effort of the will, but in the sounding forth of this wondrous story, always full of new life and fresh power; and hence, that the only means to produce faith is to open our ears to the story, and let its wondrous influence do its own work on our hearts. Most people who find a difficulty in believing are kept from it by thinking so much about their own faith. If they would never give it a thought, but transfer every thought that takes this direction to Him who is the great Object of Faith, they would soon find themselves believing almost before they knew what was befalling them.

And this leads us on to consider the case of those, and they are many, who tell us with great distress—

"*I am trying to trust Jesus, but I cannot bring myself to do it.*"

Let those who use such language reflect for a moment on its real meaning. Does it not, after all, sound somewhat startling? How should we like such words applied to ourselves? Where is there one of us, who is a servant, that would brook such an utterance from his master: "I am trying to trust you, but I cannot bring myself to do so"? I do not think we should wait in the same situation to hear that twice. But as a matter of fact, we should never think of using such language to our fellow-men, unless we regarded them as most untrustworthy. We never yet found it difficult to trust the trustworthy; and if we were once really persuaded that our blessed Lord must needs be perfectly trustworthy in that particular respect in which we put our trust in Him, whatever our experiences may be, we should soon find it easy to trust Him too.

If we had some special reason for wishing to

trust a special friend with all that we have in the world, and yet felt a little doubtful whether we could safely do so, we should never think of bringing ourselves to believe by a mere effort, of will; we should make fuller inquiries into our friend's character, and as soon as our inquiries thoroughly satisfied us that our friend was all that we could desire, we should not try to trust him, but trust him; indeed, we should feel it impossible to *try* and trust him, so spontaneous would our confidence be.

Let us, if we will, make inquiries about Him whom we are invited to trust; for faith cometh by hearing. What information do we glean as to His trustworthiness from outcast prostitute and despised publican, from cleansed leper and dying robber, from all the many who put their case into His hands? Surely all alike affirm that Jesus is trustworthy. Or let us carry our inquiries higher, for the witness of God is greater, more worthy of credit, than the witness of man; and surely His reply must needs be such as this: "I trusted My own beloved Son to win salvation for a world, and you may trust Him to save your single soul." Once let the soul grasp this comforting thought, and we shall no longer be able to "*try* and trust

Him." To all such difficulties the true answer has been given by an ancient sage : "Acquaint now thyself with Him, and be at peace, and thereby good shall come unto thee."

And at this point, if we might offer a word of advice to all who find it so very difficult to escape from their own self-consciousness, to dismiss that shadow of themselves, which ever catches the eyes, and diverts them from the Sun of Righteousness, we would say, in the words of the Psalmist, "Oh, let your song be of Him, and praise Him; and let your talking be of all His wondrous works." We have before pointed out that prayer is very useful at any earlier stage of the soul's experience, it will be found that praise is equally helpful here. The act of expressing praise and gratitude to God for the complete atonement made by Christ is one of those "works" by which "faith is made perfect;" that is to say, the soul by such a definite act commits itself to a distinct attitude of faith, shows its decision to trust, by doing that which is most natural to do when we do trust; and while thus engaged in honouring God by offering Him thanks and praise, the soul is drawn away from its own self-consciousness, and is the more disposed to regard as a reality that for which it is already expressing its gratitude. How often have we seen that the first utterance of praise has been, as it were, the signal for the emancipation of the soul from the thraldom of unbelief; the spell is broken the moment that we turn our backs upon ourselves, and begin to contemplate Him, and to " give unto the Lord the honour due unto His Name."

Only we may add, by way of caution, let no man make a sort of experiment with praise, as though it were a kind of charm or incantation, it is mere hypocrisy to praise God with a view to producing an effect upon our feelings and experi ences, while there is no doubt that when we do praise God for the proper reason, an effect on our feelings will be produced. Nor are we to regard praise as a means of cajoling the Divine Being, and insinuating ourselves into His favour, but rather as a proper acknowledgment of the favour which He has already accorded to us, and our expression of our humble willingness to accept that favour.

It is most necessary that our faith should be brought to some kind of definite expression, otherwise it wastes its energies in mere vague admissions. This end would seem to have been attained in Apostolic times by the primitive mode of employing the ordinance of Baptism. When an inquirer was really anxious to commit himself to the obedience of faith, he was immediately led to the waters of Baptism, and in the very act of submitting to this ordinance his faith was, so to speak, brought to a definite focus; and thus, in the act of Baptism, early believers saw themselves buried and raised with Christ. In dealing with those who have already been baptized, we cannot thus make use of the ordinance, but none the less is it necessary for us to seek some definite expression of faith, and we can find no better than the actual utterance of words of grateful trust, and that without any reference to our emotional experience at the moment. The gates of the Spiritual City are praise, as the walls are salvation; and they who seek to enjoy the security afforded by the walls, will do well to enter in by the appointed gates.

It will often, however, be observed that the seeking soul exhibits at this stage in its experience an obstinate and, we may almost say, dogged indisposition to utter a syllable of praise; it will readily pray or bemoan its own wretchedness, but it is held back from praise by a feeling that any such expression must needs be an act of hypocrisy. " How can I praise God when I don't feel that I have found what I am seeking?" The soul will be disposed to ask, "How can I use words that I really don't feel?" Such need to be reminded that the great work which Christ has wrought for them is not neutralized by their own unbelief; that whatever their feelings and experiences may be, it is true that God gave His Son, and it is true that Christ died for sinners and for them. They need to be brought to see that it is, to say the least of it, a strange return that we make to a Benefactor who has obtained the highest benefits for us at the gravest cost, when we tell Him that we cannot thank Him until He gives us something more. As for their not having the feeling of grateful joy, which most naturally finds expression in praise, what they have really to concern themselves with is not so much whether they *feel* gratitude as whether they *mean* gratitude. If they honestly desire to express the thanks which they feel are due, surely they are not playing the hypocrite when they open their lips and acknowledge their debt in words of thanksgiving. By such an act they will in all probability be led away from themselves, and from brooding over their own miseries, and thus will be the better able to rest their faith on Him whom they have extolled as the sinner's Saviour and theirs.

# CHAPTER XII.

## CONCLUSION.

WE noticed in our last chapter some of the forms of perplexity which are frequently encountered by the seeking soul at the very last stage of its progress towards the goal of its ardent desires—the Redeemer's cross; but those that we have referred to are only samples out of a vast army of difficulties, the mere enumeration of which would fatigue the patience of the reader, as the attempt to grapple with them often severely tests the perseverance of the spiritual guide. The battle is now almost gained, and the malignant foe has fairly to exhaust all his resources of deception, if by any means he may still retain the almost liberated soul within the mazes of his labyrinth.

Introspection, which if properly guarded has its uses at other times, is the besetting sin of the soul at this point in its experience: the man seems haunted by himself; his sins, his hardness of heart, his inability to believe, his incapacity to feel, his misery, his helplessness,—these are the subjects upon which he continues dolefully to ring the changes, forgetting apparently altogether that salvation is to be obtained by looking at Christ, and not at self. Now it is obvious that the soul cannot at one and the same moment contemplate . these two contrasted objects, Christ and self, any more than the eye can look in opposite directions at the same time. If we insist upon examining ourselves, we cannot see Christ; whereas if we look at Christ, we shall cease from examining ourselves.

It would be well if those who yield to this besetting sin would consider how, according to obvious physical laws, they are necessarily defeating the objects that they above all things desire to promote. They long for certain inward experiences, and yet at the same time preclude themselves from enjoying these by insisting on examining and analyzing whatever experiences they have. He who is thus employed is like a child running after its own shadow: that which he examines must ever melt away in his examination of it, and the reason is plain. These experiences are states of consciousness, and the examination of them is an act of consciousness; but the more our moral consciousness is taken up with the act, in the exercise of our critical faculty, the less of moral consciousness is there left for the state. The proper feelings may be there, and yet we may be prevented from detecting them, because our consciousness is preoccupied in the attempt to detect. For example, peace is a state of consciousness, and one that may have already begun to exist without our notice being very forcibly drawn to it; but any attempt to search ourselves as to whether we have peace, is an act of consciousness requiring so considerable an exercise of our faculties, that our attention cannot fail to be so taken up with that, as to leave little or no moral consciousness for the state of experience to be examined. In other words, the feeling of peace is lost because all our thoughts are absorbed in the attempt to discover it.

This simple law of our nature accounts for the fact that seeking souls who are really in earnest often weary themselves in a futile endeavour to find peace where we should have expected, from their evident sincerity and determination, that they would have obtained the desired blessing at once.

This frame of mind is betrayed by many almost stereotyped phrases, which are familiar to all who have endeavoured to carry on evangelizing work. Here are some of them :—

    " *How can I believe when I have no feeling of peace or joy ?* "

To which it might be enough to reply, How can you have any feeling of peace and joy when you do not believe? Peace and joy are the names we give to certain states of consciousness, and are induced by intelligible causes. When the soul has committed itself into a trustworthy Saviour's hands, it has His own work and His own word to assure it of security ; all the causes of fear and misgiving are eliminated, and peace and joy are the natural and necessary effects; but so long as our attitude towards God is not one of simple childlike trust, there is a controversy between us and Him, we are still under the ban of His wrath, and must remain in that condition until we submit to the obedience of faith. How is it possible that we can possess peace and joy when the state of our relations with God is such as must necessarily cause inward disquiet and distress? We have nothing to do with joy and peace, but to enjoy these blessed experiences when God is pleased to grant them to us ; it is no part of our duty to endeavour directly to induce them. Joy and peace are reckoned by St. Paul amongst the fruits of the Spirit : we may trust Him to produce these where He Himself has been received ; what we have to see to is that we have received Him, and St. Paul teaches us plainly that He is to be received by the hearing of faith (Gal. iii. 2).

Neither do our peace and joy commend us to God, nor are they the basis of our confidence with respect to our own safety, and it seems more than probable that God in His wisdom often has to deny them to seeking souls, for a time at any rate, just because He well knows our disposition to put them in the wrong place, or to trust to them. As a matter of fact, this abuse of God's gifts does not unfrequently occur; when He who deals with men in different ways, suiting His treatment to their case, is pleased, as He often is, to give an extra-ordinary sense of rapture or of repose, the soul concludes that all must now be well, simply because it is happy, and by-and-by, when the happy feelings have subsided, it finds itself without any solid basis for its confidence, and probably relapses into de-spondency. We are persuaded that this is the cause of by far the greater part of the backsliding and apostacy which often follows an extensive religious movement : awakened souls mistake excited emotions for intelligent, heartfelt faith; and when the excitement passes away, they find that they have "no root in themselves." Closely analogous to this is another complaint very frequently heard on the lips of a seeking soul :

" *I cannot feel any love to Christ; my heart is cold and insensible.*"

We would like to ask those who are exercised upon this point where they find the doctrine of *iustification by love* revealed in Holy Scripture. But if they are not to be justified by love, what have they to do with examining and scrutinizing their love to Christ at this stage in their experience ? Do they desire to win God's love to themselves by the display of theirs to Him ? if so, they are exactly inverting the true order of things. God wins our love to Him by displaying His love to us. Let such persons ask themselves whether they ever contrived to call love for any earthly object into existence by introspection—whether it is not rather the case that we may easily persuade ourselves by a process of introspection that we have no real affections for our dearest and closest friends. Love is the child of faith. Whom we do not trust we cannot love, and nothing would be more strange than that men should be able to love such a being as the morbid imaginations of anxious souls too often present to their own minds as God. A capricious, unsympathetic tyrant, who delights in demanding impossibilities, and in tantalizing us with offers that he has no ·intention we should accept, who is always specially hard upon the bruised reed, mercilessly criticises the character and quality of the faith of which he is the object— such a being is scarcely likely to elicit, by the mere manifestation of his charms, the enthusiastic love and devotion of the human heart.

Let us be thankful that so hideous an idol god exists only in the diseased imagination of his worshippers; but if these complain of the absence of all feelings of love from their heart, let us implore them to turn their back upon the Juggernaut under whose wheels they have been endeavouring to imolate themselves, and begin to believe in a God whose nature and whose name is *Love*, and who having given the strongest possible proof of His love on the cross, is now equally prepared, with Himself, freely to give us all things. If, instead of thinking about our love, we were to ponder on His love to us, we should soon find ourselves filled with love, as well as with peace and joy ; but how manv strangle love, as it were, at its very birth, by admitting a fatal suspicion, a shadow of unbelief, into their heart. Trust fully, and the more you trust, the more you will love. But here is another branch from the same parent stem,

"*I do believe in Christ, but I don't feel any different.*"

We have here illustrated by such a sentence a species of religious empiricism. As a medical empiricist gives a dose, and then carefully examines the effects, so the man whom we are now considering proceeds to try experiment after experiment upon the faithfulness of God, and with far from satisfactory results. Had one of the bitten Israelites of old gone to his tent door with the distinct idea of trying the experiment whether or not there was anything in the vaunted brazen serpent, and had he proceeded to fix his gaze in alternation first on the serpent and then on his swollen limb, to see whether any good had been effected, can we for a moment suppose that such unbelief would have been rewarded by a cure? no more probable is it that he who makes an experiment upon the cross of Christ will find the experiment a successful one. The wounded

Israelite looked with the full persuasion that God's appointed cure must cure him, and we are to trust Christ with equal confidence that God's appointed remedy for sin must be a remedy indeed. Do not let us make Him a liar by setting up our feelings against His word. When we have ceased to make our feelings the test of God's faithfulness, we shall find that in many very important respects we do feel very different, when once our souls are fully trusted into the hands of Christ. We shall then begin to feel what we want, when we have decided to trust God, without reference to our feelings. Here is another and very frequent form that such difficulties take,

"*I do believe in Christ, and I feel in some respects better than I did, but still I don't feel that I am saved.*"

Of such the question may be asked, Would you rather *be safe* without feeling safe, or feel safe without being safe? If your common sense forces you to prefer the former of these alternatives, then you may comfort yourself that this exactly describes your condition, if what you say is true, *i.e.*, that you really do believe in Christ; for whether you feel safe or not, Christ is responsible for the safety of those who trust themselves to Him. But before

such trouble themselves any more about "*feeling*
that they are saved," it will be well for them to ask
whether they *know* that by grace they are saved?
Here it will generally be found there is equal
uncertainty, and so we travel back towards the
root of the evil; if you do not know that you are
saved, why do you not know? One of two
answers alone can be given to this inquiry, either
that the word which assures us that if we believe
on the Lord Jesus Christ we shall be saved, that
he that believeth hath everlasting life, and so forth,
must have proved false in this particular instance,
or else that the soul does not really believe and
know that it believes in Christ. The latter of
these two alternatives is the only one that we are
prepared to accept, and accepting that, the whole
thing is explained. The soul does not really
believe; that is to say, it does not leave itself
regardless of its feelings in the hands of Christ,
and hence it is not safe, but it desires, without
doing this, to feel safe, which would be to feel safe
when it is not safe; therefore it is really seeking to
feel safe without being safe, instead of making sure
of being safe without reference to feeling safe.
Here, as in other cases, the fault lies in the
absence of full confidence in Christ. For if I

honestly am persuaded that my full moral confidence is reposed on Him, I have every right to be equally persuaded that what I have committed to Him is safe in His keeping.

While putting this as plainly as we can, we will seize this opportunity of protesting, as strongly as it is possible for us to do, against that slanderous misrepresentation of the evangelist's position which is sometimes made, even by intelligent and well-informed persons. We have heard it asserted that the teaching of those who believe in present salvation amounts to this, " Believe that you are saved, and saved you will be." This might well be described as the gospel of nonsense ; and if any people are silly enough to believe in it or teach it, they must certainly be capable of qualifying as high priests in the temple of Folly. But does any one really maintain a position so extravagant as this, that you must believe a lie to make it become the truth ? Not such, at any rate, has been the Gospel preached in recent and prominent evangelizing efforts ; not such, certainly, was the Gospel of the New Testament.

Our message is, " Believe in the Saviour, and then, because He is a Saviour, know that you are saved." Salvation is by no means contingent upon our knowledge of it, but our knowledge of it naturally flows from conscious compliance with its conditions ; and therefore, where the knowledge is absent, we not unreasonably conclude that the conditions cannot have been consciously complied with. It probably will be found in all such cases that the soul has been content with a general and vague belief that Christ is the Saviour of the world, and therefore its Saviour, instead of resting in Him as its Saviour, and setting Him and the provision of His grace against every doubt and fear and misgiving that the consciousness of sin may suggest to the mind. The feeling that I am saved, if it is not to be misleading, must arise from my knowledge of the fact that I am saved, and this again is dependent upon my inward consciousness of trust in my Saviour. To revert for a moment to a figure I have before employed, the man that was drowning, but who accepts the deliverance offered to him by one whom he knows to be able and willing to save him, is saved the moment he consciously trusts to his deliverer. He knows he is saved, because he knows that he has trusted a trustworthy deliverer; but all his sensible experiences, as he is being drawn through deep water, may seem to give the lie to his knowledge : his reasonable conviction says safety, his nervous timidity, in other words, his feelings, say danger. Under these circumstances he will resolutely set his knowledge against his feelings, until the latter, being unsupported by facts, that is, being deprived of their cause, have to consent to be calmed into tranquillity. So the feeling of safety will necessarily sooner or later follow, not from any attempt to create it, but from the elimination of all causes of an opposite conclusion.

*" But I am afraid, when the excitement is over, I shall be just as I was before."*

This depends upon what has really taken place. If you have merely been stirred and excited, then probably your last state will even be worse than your first; but if you have taken God for your salvation, and Christ for your life, surely all things have now become new. Before, God was a Being you feared and shrank from; His commands were fetters of legal restraint, and His service was a burden; now He is your reconciled Father, to whom you have freedom of access through the rent Veil. You have found out that He loves you, and are therefore sure that He will call you to nothing but what is for your highest good and happiness. Whatever you may be called to do or to suffer, you will find now that His grace is sufficient for you. You have begun to live by Him, and it will be your blessed privilege to draw all your resources from Him, who is the same yesterday, and to-day, and for ever. You have no right to be apprehensive about the future, for this is one form of unbelief: as we trust our past, so let us trust our present and our future to Him. Surely if He can say, " Thy sins be forgiven thee," He can also say, " Rise up and walk." If He has taught us to take no thought about the morrow, in worldly matters, for " sufficient to the day is the evil thereof," surely He would have us equally uncareful with respect to the spiritual trials and difficulties that may be before us. You are not asked to make a strenuous resolution to lead a new and different life, but rather to confess your inability to do so, and then to trust God to accomplish in you that which you cannot do for yourself. A similar difficulty often finds expression thus,

" *I don't like to make a profession, for fear I should go back from it, and bring discredit on the cause of God.*"

How natural and plausible this sounds ! and yet what have we here but the very quintessence of unbelief? We profess to have trusted Christ, and therefore to have received from Him His unspeakable gift; we know that He who gave, alone can keep us possessed of what He has given, but we are afraid of letting it be known that we have received the gift, for fear it should prove that it has only been given to be withdrawn. Does God thus mock us with a histrionic display of benevolence which is in danger of evaporating in air as soon as its professed gifts are exposed to any definite test of worth?

Now, as if to guard us against such a snare, God has bound together belief and confession in such wise that man cannot put them asunder. The ancient preachers of the Gospel claimed (and so do our modern missionaries) that their converts should not only believe with their hearts, but confess with their mouths, and submit to Baptism as an open confession of their faith. In confirmation, where it is what it ought to be,—the expression of whole-hearted surrender of ourselves to Christ,—a similar opportunity is offered by our own Church to those who have been baptized in infancy. This is too often also a mere hollow form, but still it witnesses to the importance and necessity of confession. In whatever way, however, the confession is made, made it must be, for the promise of salvation is conditional upon not only the inward exercise but the outward expression of faith, and this has been ordained, no doubt, for the very reason, amongst others, on account of which we have supposed the soul to be shrinking from it. You shrink from confessing Christ, because you are afraid you may fall. God calls upon you to confess Christ, that you may be brought definitely to trust Him to keep you from falling. It is a strange way of showing our trust in Christ as Saviour, to proceed at once to distrust Christ as Preserver. Let us trust Christ altogether, or not at all.

*"I do believe, and I hope I am saved, but I have not full assurance."*

What do we mean by full assurance? To return to our figure of the drowning man, wherein would his full assurance of safety consist? Surely in his setting his conviction of the ability and willingness of his deliverer to save him against every thought, feeling, or experience suggesting an opposite conclusion, so that every doubt and fear should be completely mastered and neutralized. Similarly we surely have full assurance when we reply to all inward suggestions of disquietude or alarm, " I know whom I have believed, and am persuaded that He is able to keep that which I have committed to Him against that day." The writer of the Epistle to the Hebrews uses the word which we render " full assurance," just in the way in which we should expect it to be used in Holy Scripture, *i.e.*, as descriptive of an attitude of soul arising from the contemplation of the provisions of grace, "having boldness to enter by a new and living way by the blood of Jesus .... and having a high priest .... let us draw near with a true heart, in full assurance of faith." The same word is used by St. Luke in the beginning of his Gospel, where he speaks of the things which are most surely believed amongst us; and St. Paul speaks of Abraham (using the same word) as being fully persuaded that what God promised He was able to perform.

It will be observed that in all these cases no reference is made to any extraordinary inward experience, or to any sign or mysterious token of God's favour, but to a well-grounded conviction resting upon the known character of the Divine Being. Such an assurance as this is surely within our reach, if we respond to the leadings of the Holy Spirit, and fix our soul's gaze upon the Lamb of God. But perhaps the difficulty takes a somewhat different form—

"*I do believe, but I have not the witness of the Spirit.*"

Those who are troubled on this point must remember that God the Holy Ghost does not deal with all in the same way, and that it is possible to form an erroneous idea of the way in which He will manifest His presence, even as did the Jews in their expectation of Messiah. Even so we may fail to recognize His testimony on account of our false preconceptions respecting it. There are doubtless cases in which the witness of the Spirit is so clearly distinct. from every other experience, that those to whom it is granted could doubt the testimony of their sense as readily as they could the Divine influence, but there are other cases in which the Spirit's witness is to be found rather in the change of desires and the consciousness of new inclinations, than in any extraordinary and apparently supernatural manifestations.

One thing the Holy Spirit ever does witness to in each heart that He enters, and that is our sonship. He teaches us to cry Abba, Father. God is to us, His reconciled children, no longer a dim abstraction, no longer a cause of terror, a Judge from whose frown we shrink, or a severe Master before whose rebuke we quail, but the Father of mercies and the God of all consolation, into whose presence we enter without fear through that grace wherein we stand. We are persuaded that many who complain that they have not the witness of the Spirit are perfectly conscious of this change in their relations with God; and if they desire a further testimony, they will do well to remember that there are three that bear witness on earth, the Spirit and the Water and the Blood, and to strengthen their confidence by accepting the witness of all, instead of confining their attention to the single testimony.

The ordinance of Baptism is God's appointed witness to the cleansing from sin of every true believer, and to his union with Christ in His death and resurrection, so that to us Baptism is as much "a seal of the righteousness that is by faith," as Circumcision was to Isaac, though he had received the rite as an unconscious infant. Perhaps in our evangelistic teaching we do not make enough of this divinely appointed assurance of pardon and acceptance, on which every true believer has a perfect right to fall back with absolute confidence.

And then there is the witness of the blood. Our assurance of present salvation does not rest merely upon a number of texts, but upon the great fact of the Atonement. If the life of Christ freely given has been accepted by God Himself as an expiation for human guilt, forgiveness and justification cannot but follow when we accept what God has accepted. To doubt our present salvation when we are resting on Christ and His finished work, is to impugn the efficacy of the Atonement, and to question the value of that outpoured Life, of which we so well sing that—

> "Jesus' blood, through earth and skies,
> Mercy—free, boundless mercy—cries."

We have followed with patient steps the seeking soul in its progress through the tangled maze which an enemy has erected around the cross of Christ. And here our task ceases. It is not for us to attempt to describe here the happier experiences which ensue when at last, it may be *at long last*, the soul finds itself under the shadow of this great rock in a weary land. We would only remind our readers that when these difficulties have been surmounted, and the ransomed soul has learnt to sing, " Behold, God is my salvation; I will trust, and not be afraid," it has then reached the beginning, not the end, of true Christian experience. Then it is that we find ourselves in a position to value and make use of the appointed means of grace, and with joy to draw water out of the wells of salvation. Nor can we bring this volume to a close without pointing out how much, humanly speaking, must depend upon the way in which the new-born soul is nurtured and trained by those who by the providence of God occupy to him the position of spiritual guides.

How many an earnest young Christian is lost to our Church, and forfeits all the special and, I may say, unspeakable benefits that under God our Church has to offer, just because he does not meet with spiritual sympathy or wise encouragement from the parochial clergyman, or perhaps because he finds no provision made to meet the spiritual wants which specially belong to this stage of spiritual experiences. The Apostle fed his young converts with milk, and not with strong meat, even though their actual age as believers might have justified him in providing a more substantial diet. We fear that an opposite course is not unfrequently pursued by his less skilful followers, and that many a young Christian is so nearly choked by the severe nutriment of sound but somewhat dry doctrinal teaching, or of terribly regular and orderly liturgical services, that he is fain to seek a little "pure milk" at the first Wesleyan chapel he can find his way into.

What young believers need is, *first*, definite personal spirituality in him who is to be their pastor. Without this he cannot hope to influence them, nor is it well that he should. We have our Lord's own authority for saying that a stranger His sheep will not follow, for they know not the voice of a stranger. *Second*, warm and tender sympathy, shown in readiness to understand and enter into all the usual trials of early Christian experience; *third*, wise and gentle firmness, employed in directing the spiritual child to that which is likely to be wholesome, and in diverting him from what might become injurious; *fourth*, a sufficient supply of such means as are likely to cherish and develop the spiritual life at this stage. Amongst these, we would set first that blessed ordinance which is suited alike for the new-born babe and for the father in Christ. It is a great point, surely, that in most churches now, when an earnest work is being carried on, young Christians can enjoy the inestimable privilege of a weekly communion. For this, no doubt, such will require to be trained and taught, for fear it should become a mere formal habit, and so degenerate into a superstition; but if they learn the true uses of this holy ordinance, they will find in it a most real and valuable help, and one that will not be equally within their reach outside the Church in which God has cast their lot. Next to this we would point out the importance of more informal helps—Bible-classes, prayer-meetings, and meetings for fellowship and mutual help, prayer-unions, and communicants' unions, and other means, of which our space will not allow us to speak particularly. And, we would add, few things will be found more helpful than occasional private interviews with those who have professed to come to Christ, in the clergyman's own study, which should be used as a consulting room two or three evenings at least every week. *Fifth*, the young Christian will need to be judiciously trained to work for his Master, not thrust to the front too soon, but kept well in hand, and helped and guided in the use of any gifts he may possess. We cannot expect Christians to grow or be healthy unless they are kept busy; and the Master has left *to every man his work.*

But we must end. If these pages enable any spiritual guide to deal more efficiently with those who inquire of him "What must I do to be saved?"

or if they are used by God the Holy Ghost to clear up the difficulties of any earnest seeker after Christ, and to point the way to the Cross, they will not have been written in vain.    In the hope that this may be so, we now commit them into His hands, who has never said " Seek ye My face " in vain ; trusting that He may use them to show to some, at any rate, that " His love unknown has broken every barrier down," and that any difficulties that yet remain are of our own creation.

**THE END.**

Lightning Source UK Ltd.
Milton Keynes UK
UKOW06f1922200815

257277UK00012B/213/P

9 781330 117347